HOTEL Humor AND Hospitality HINTS

I highly recommend this book to anyone interested in pursuing a career in the hospitality industry. You will find it interesting, informative, insightful and amusing. Her stories involving hotel staff and guests make you feel as if you were there. You will certainly benefit from the helpful hints and coaching tips provided at the end of selected chapters.

—**BOB JEHLI**, more than thirty years in hotel and conference center management, most recently as the Director of Operations at the American Airlines Training and Conference Center

This may be the author's first book, but her passion and love for the hospitality industry is real and present in this very insightful and entertaining book! Whether you are a student majoring in hospitality or a seasoned road warrior, you'll find yourself amused and possibly shocked by the daily occurrences that are presented to the front desk—and scratching your head. Can these stories actually be true!? After working in the industry for forty-two years, I can assure you that when working in a hotel, anything is possible at any time.

If you're considering a career in the hospitality industry, you've been warned—you won't be bored, but you can have a very rewarding and fulfilling career! As an added bonus, don't forget to read the very insightful Hospitality Hints.

—**GLENN ROBBINS**, retired Regional Director with one of the largest global hotel chains in the world

It is immediately evident that the heart and contents of this excellent book could be turned into a training manual for any service organization worldwide. Kim provides a personal and inspirational touch to each chapter—priceless advice! The stories reflect her non-negotiables that protect travelers. Moments of truth along with temptations and tests and humor. The quips and tips are based on her love of human connection, civility, and kindness—everyday insights that lead to action: "quick to hear, slow to speak, and slow to anger." Kim closes saying, "every property has its uniqueness and attractions, but it is the people that keep guests coming back." How true!

—**RITA M. MURRAY**, PhD and **RONALD MURRAY**, Performance Consulting, LLC

As a road warrior for most of my career, I've experienced the ups and downs of the hospitality industry. Wonderful professionals who treated me like family, with only an occasional sourpuss. I've long been curious about what goes on behind the desk. How is it possible to be ever-friendly, welcoming the weary traveler—and guests who often try their patience?

Kimberly Annington, a hospitality management veteran, answers these questions and many more in her book *Hotel Humor and Hospitality Hints*. The stories run from the ridiculous (the elephant who came to the wedding) to the tragic (a guest who transitioned from this life to the next in one of their rooms). Annington paints an intriguing look into the profession she loves and shares it with the travelers who, like me, want to know the inside scoop.

A delightful read featuring short chapters that beg you to "read just one more" before retiring for the night. Great pick for travelers, hospitality professionals, and those preparing for a hotelier career.

—**DEB DEARMOND**, road warrior extraordinaire

Hotel Humor AND Hospitality Hints

SECRETS FROM BEHIND THE FRONT DESK

KIMBERLY ANNINGTON

KAE
PRESS

Hotel Humor and Hospitality Hints

©2023 by Kimberly Annington
www.hotelhumor-hints.com

Paperback ISBN: 979-8-9864038-0-9
E-book ISBN: 979-8-9864038-1-6
Audiobook ISBN: 979-8-9864038-2-3
Hardcover ISBN: 979-8-9864038-3-0

Published by KAE Press

This work of non-fiction reflects the author's present recollections of experiences over time. All names, with the exception of Kimberly Annington, Sharon Tedford, Gareth Tedford and Deb DeArmond, have been changed to protect identity of people mentioned. Business names and locations have been changed, some events have been compressed, and some dialogue has been recreated.

Illustrations and cover image by B.K. Taylor

Edited by Michelle Rayburn

Cover design and typesetting by Michelle Rayburn

Audiobook production by Sharon Tedford

Special thanks to Deb DeArmond for writing her story and granting permission to publish it in the chapter "A Walk on the Wild Side."

Special thanks to Sharon Tedford for sharing your story and granting permission to publish it in the chapter "A Not-So-Suite Upgrade."

To Lucia. What a difference you've made in my life.

Contents

Acknowledgments

Thank you, to the One from whom every good gift comes.

Thank you, Lucia, for listening to my stories and laughing with me over the years. Thank you for encouraging me to write this book.

Sharon, thank you for introducing me to Deb and for helping me along by letting her know I "had a book in my head." And thank you for the time you spent as a beta reader extraordinaire and audiobook producer!

Thank you both for helping to make a dream come true.

Deb DeArmond, you are an amazing lady! This book would not have happened without you. Thank you for believing in me and coaching me in such a way that was always edifying. I look forward to every meeting with you. You have taught me so much.

BK, you caught the vision for my book from the start. Thank you for the outstanding illustrations. It has been a pleasure working with you and laughing with you.

Michelle Rayburn, you are an expert in your field! I enjoyed working with you immensely. You made the process so easy and stress-free! Thank you for the editing, design, and publishing help.

Thank you to my fellow hoteliers with whom I have worked over the years. Especially my work family (you know who you are). It has been a true delight. You've made this book possible.

Thank you to my family and loved ones. Thank you, Christie, Melina, Natalie, and Wade, for being excited with me. Thank you,

Gracia, for the technical help and input. Thank you, Charlotte, for brainstorming with me. Thank you, Pat and Mr. Allen, for being an encouragement to me. Thank you to my dad, Coady, and to Ms. Chris for wanting to be the first to receive a copy of this book.

Introduction

This book is for everyone who enjoys a humorous story or is curious about what goes on behind the scenes in a hotel—employee and guest alike. If you are a hospitality student, this will enrich your learning and add a little fun to your academic teachings.

My hospitality career started at age twenty. I worked at the front desk of a motel attached to a major fast-food restaurant. After one year, I moved on to a full-service hotel and have been in full service ever since. I worked my way up through the ranks and plateaued as a department-head manager, an intentional strategy for me to maintain a good balance between work and personal life. With thirty years in the industry in four hotels, I spent twenty-five of those years at one property. Most of the stories I share are from that hotel. Front office management is my specialty, and reservations is a close runner-up.

The two things I love most about the industry are the home-like atmosphere and that being kind to others is a critically important part of the job. Hotels have a man or woman of the house—the GM—and they have a kitchen and many warm beds for sleeping. How much closer to a home atmosphere can you get? Few other jobs boast the same. Our homes and jobs are what we make them, and with effort and intentionality, both can be a wonderful place to spend our time.

Year after year, I have shared hilarious or unbelievable stories with my family and friends. Now I want to share them with you. So, whether you are a student, a traveler, or both, you can laugh with me as I recount some of my most memorable interactions and experiences. As a bonus, each chapter includes especially useful hospitality hints.

For the Student

I encourage you to work part-time in the industry while in school. There is no substitute for experience. While getting your feet wet, seek out a mentor. A good manager loves to train and nurture someone eager to learn. Express to them your desire to grow.

In addition to your mentor, allow me to take you under my wing and share tips and insights that will help launch your career. Take great strides forward as you laugh with me and read unexaggerated accounts from my years in the industry. Learn how to always take the high road no matter what the situation. Discover how to continue to advance through the ranks by having a consistent management style.

You will learn to manage with ease and prevent guests and fellow employees from pushing your buttons. Upon graduation, you'll have book knowledge that will serve you well. From reading *Hotel Humor and Hospitality Hints*, you'll gain added understanding and insight from my real-world experience.

For the Traveler

Do you scratch your head and wonder why things happen in hotels? Do you sometimes wish situations could be different? *Hotel Humor and Hospitality Hints* is the perfect book for snuggling up with at the end of your day. Come close as I share behind-the-scenes funnies and follies as well as the more serious side of the business. Learn what the manager you just spoke to goes through in a day. It will give you a new perspective. Use that new perspective the next time you walk through a hotel's front door, especially if there's a complication. If you hope to have a problem solved in your favor, the way you speak to that person has a big impact. Hotel employees love to assist and even go out of their way for a kind guest.

I could have written a book about what I don't like or the dark side of the industry, but that isn't where I place my focus. I seek the good, the fun, the funny. It's all around us. If you seek it, you will find it. Attitude is a choice and affects everything we do.

Hospitality is indeed an art. There are no static rules to follow when interacting with guests. We must use our good judgment to ensure we handle every interaction to each particular guest's satisfaction. And the same goes for the traveler—there are lessons to be learned here as well.

No matter how sophisticated, posh, or simple your hotel, and no matter what state or country you're in, the principles in this book apply to you.

What goes on behind the front desk? What makes some hoteliers more proficient than others? Read on. I dare you not to laugh.

1

Here We Go Again

As a new twenty-something front desk supervisor at my second property, I didn't realize how vital work relationships were. Until it was too late.

Glen, my new manager of six months, approached me as I clocked in for my shift. He asked to speak with me in what used to be our Human Resources office, a recently eliminated department. As we walked down the hall, I wished him a happy birthday.

He mumbled something and continued to walk ahead of me.

We stepped into the office where Jared, Glen's new assistant, looked our way, blank-faced.

This must be a meeting about a new procedure or employee issue.

Glen rounded the desk to sit down.

"Have a seat, Kim." He motioned to the chair next to Jared's.

Glen opened the conversation and got right to the point. "Kim, you know that you and I have had our differences. Well, Jared and I have talked, and I've decided it's just not working out between us. We're going to have to let you go."

As his words hit me, the room grew dim. All I could see clearly was Glen in front of me. My hearing muffled. I gripped the chair to fight off the shock.

Let me go? I turned to Jared.

He nodded his head. "It's mutual, Kim."

I looked him squarely in the eye. "Glen, what are you saying? We've had minor differences, but I had no idea it would come to this."

I tried to make sense of what was happening. *I have worked here six years with a clean HR record. I have never received disciplinary action. I get along with everyone. I'm dedicated, and I know I do a good job. I've even received awards. How can he roadblock me from simply going upstairs to work as I always do?*

I searched for something to say. Glen's actions weren't right, and I knew it. But I didn't know how to defend myself.

"Glen, you could have at least let me know this was coming or given me other options."

Without vocalizing it, I speculated that Glen's friend, who had followed him to the hotel, was waiting in the wings to be promoted.

After a few minutes of trying to gain understanding, I realized there was nothing I could do or say to change his mind, and the hotel had no HR manager I could consult. Glen decided we didn't work well together, and that was it. My time at this hotel was over.

Within two weeks, I started work at a new property in a city neighboring my previous hotel. No supervisor positions were available, so I started as a front desk agent. On my first day of work, Christian Hansen, the general manager, said it made his day to welcome me aboard. A few years prior, we'd worked together at the place where I'd been unceremoniously (and unfairly) dismissed.

I had been at my new property for about three months when I received a call from Jared at the other hotel. He apologized for his involvement in my firing. He explained he couldn't stand to work with Glen any longer. He confirmed Glen's friend did, in fact, step into my former position, and things over there were a mess.

Jared asked if my hotel, specifically the front desk, had an open position. We did. I informed HR of his interest and asked them to interview Jared as if we were not associated. I didn't know him well and wanted fairness for us both.

After a successful interview process, Jared received the position, and we worked on the same front desk team again. I was a supervisor; he was an assistant manager. One year later, his manager terminated his employment, citing a lack of leadership.

Two years later, I held the title of assistant front office manager at the same property. Everything was going just fine, thank you very much, until the day our HR director, Angela, called me at home.

"Kim, I need to talk to you about something. Are you sitting down?" She sounded tentative.

"Yes. I'm sitting down. What's up?" Now I was uncomfortable.

"Glen Samson is joining our team. He's going to be our new assistant general manager."

"Glen Samson?" The broom that was in my hand hit the floor.

Angela's continued explanation convinced me she was serious. This was no joke.

"No, Angela!" *He can't follow me here. Who fires someone, then follows them?*

Angela reassured me. "It will be okay. You both are more mature and experienced now."

I pleaded with Angela to no avail.

Giving in, I sank back into my chair. "It will be fine. You're right. We're both more mature now. When does Glen start?"

"In two weeks."

I thanked her for the information, then hung up the phone, feeling defeated.

I want to continue working at the hotel, but I don't want him there.

On Glen's first day of work, I welcomed him as my new manager. I gave him the respect his position deserved. Although we never spoke of what happened at the previous property, we established a friendly working relationship—an essential step to a successful effort the second time around.

Angela was right. We were both more mature and experienced. I knew how to handle Glen's personality better. My standoffish stance with him at the other hotel was hard on him, and his management style was hard on me. We both could have handled the situation better. And this time, we would.

After one year at the hotel, Glen transferred to another property. Admittedly, I was relieved when he moved on but also glad that we parted on good terms this time.

Hospitality Hints

❖ Value and grow work relationships. Be a positive influence.

❖ Know that management styles are different. No manager is perfect.

❖ During conflict (it will happen), be introspective. What will *you* do differently?

❖ Never burn your bridges. You might work with your former boss again. Or two of them, for that matter.

❖ Don't hold grudges.

❖ Help your team be their best. Talk to them and get to know them. Disciplinary action should never catch them off guard. They should see it coming a mile away.

❖ Communicate clearly with individual employees. Try to help before considering extreme disciplinary action. Zig Zigler's book *Top Performance: How to Develop Excellence in Yourself and Others*[1] is an excellent resource on this subject and more.

2

When Things Appear
Different than They Are

Sometimes things are not what they appear to be. One guest found this out the hard way.

Every so often, a first-time guest with a keen sense of smell will approach the front desk to check in and, before saying anything else, will declare, "You have a pool here."

With eyebrows raised and a grin, I reply, "Why, yes, we do. It's just down the hall."

"I knew it! I smelled the chlorine the second I walked in the door."

The indoor pool is the center of attention at our property. With its entrance door located halfway down our main corridor at the bottom of the open staircase, it's literally in the center of everything. The two-story vaulted glass walls make it impossible for passersby to miss, whether they're on the first floor or the lower level. As I walk down the hall, it's always a welcome distraction for me to look over at the pool or beyond and gaze out the window at our lush green lawn and professional-grade tennis courts.

This featured hotel amenity is enjoyed not only by our guests but also by city residents who hold a membership to our sports club.

I will never forget one club member—Dr. Splasher. He used our indoor pool daily for exercise. Afterward, he would go to work at the local hospital. The familiar routine of seeing him nearly every day somehow comforted me. I couldn't hold back a grin every time I walked down the hall and saw his dramatic, one-man commotion in the pool. The doctor's head was barely above water. He always wore headphones covered with a baggie to keep them dry. His long arms flailed as he treaded. The deep end knew the fury of his splashes. He took up that entire portion of the pool, dousing anyone within reach.

Because of his unusual swimming technique, I asked our sports club supervisor, Sheila, about the doctor.

"Kim, that's Alan Jones. He's a doctor. We call him Dr. Splasher." She giggled. "He was a runner, but it was hard on his knees, so now he treads water instead because it's low impact."

According to Sheila, Dr. Splasher had been a member long before I started work at the hotel.

I loved my coworker's cheerful Australian accent, which made her version of the story even more enjoyable.

"And you know what's funny?" She drew closer.

"Sometimes people try to *save* him," she whispered with a giggle.

My brow furrowed. "Save him?"

She nodded. "Yeah. Some people think he's drowning, so they jump in and try to save him." Her face squinted as she giggled.

"Oh. You've got to be kidding me." I stifled a laugh, then leaned in for more.

"No. I'm serious," Sheila whispered. "It's the funniest thing. Just the other day, three male guests, on a break from their meeting, were walking through the pool area to go outside to the sun deck, and one of them thought he was drowning. So, the guest jumped in, fully clothed. Tie, dress shirt, everything. Of course, he was embarrassed when he figured out the doctor didn't need help."

"I should say so. Poor guy." I shook my head. *And how startling that must have been for the doctor.*

As unbelievable as it was, I liked the fact that guests were willing to help.

Despite the occasional rescue attempt, Dr. Splasher continued to enjoy our pool for a few more years. Then one day, it dawned on me that I hadn't seen him for several weeks. So, I asked about him again.

"Sheila, is everything okay with Dr. Splasher?"

She gave a doleful smile. "Oh, Kim, he installed a pool at his house. He doesn't come here any longer."

My countenance dropped. "Oh really?"

"Yeah." She sighed and shrugged her shoulders. "He figured he would save a lot of time before work to have his own pool."

"Oh, I'm sorry to hear that, but a smart move on his part."

Dr. Splasher was part of the life of our hotel for many years. He is part of our history.

Though I never met him, I miss him.

Hospitality Hints

❖ Appreciate long-term guests and club members. Get to know them if possible. You will miss their familiar routine when they are suddenly gone.

3

Which Is More
Romantic? You Decide

Guests ask the darndest things. I knew his question was not literal. But what was he was asking?

Kim, I need you to work today. Shelly called in sick." My manager, Jill, broke the news to me over the phone. Her tone was adamant.

I knew it was my duty as a new supervisor to be a go-to person for such tasks. "I understand. I'll be there within the hour, Jill."

I had planned to spend my day poolside with a good book. That would have to wait.

I left my pool bag by the door, changed clothes, then dashed off to work.

Jill thanked me as I walked into the office. I dropped my purse and went straight to the front desk. It wasn't a busy day, so I would work alone for the next eight hours. I didn't mind, really. There are much worse places I could be on a day off.

A few hours into my shift, while I stood at the front desk still dreaming of a lazy day at the pool, a young man around my age briskly approached.

"Can you show me a romantic handhold?"

I looked up from my computer. *Is he talking to me?* I looked around. There was no one else in the area.

He drew closer. *Okay, yes, he is talking to me.*

At that moment, I thanked God for this random question that had just dropped into my day. I needed humor, and by reading his demeanor, I had a feeling this was headed there.

Where are you going with this?

I smiled. "Hello."

He asked again, "Can you show me a romantic handhold?"

Puzzled, I grinned. "Show you a romantic handhold?"

"My wife and I"—he motioned across the lobby—"are in a debate over which is more romantic. This?" He held his own hands, palms together. "Or this?" He clasped his hands together again, intertwining his fingers.

About that time, his beautiful wife approached. She stopped a short distance away with her arms folded and a playful smirk on her face.

He looked at her with eyebrows raised and head tilted back. "I'm getting another opinion."

I watched them go back and forth like it was a tennis match. Then the couple turned and looked at me expectantly.

Oh. I straightened up. *You want me to decide?*

I paused briefly to consider his question, then spoke sincerely. "You know . . ." *This is a little awkward.* "I think it might have more to do with the heart than the hands. But since you asked, I think it's this." I joined my hands and held them, palms together.

"See? I told you!" his wife exclaimed in triumph. Then she looked at me and tilted her head. "Thank you."

I turned to him and smiled apologetically. "Sorry."

He walked toward his wife, and they drifted toward the lobby in continued debate. I returned to my duties at the desk. I shook my head and laughed at the fun moment that lifted my day.

Minutes later, I looked up to see the loving couple walking across the lobby, then out the front door, holding hands—palms together.

I smiled. It had become a day I was grateful not to miss. And it's a good thing I was there. I may have just saved that man from a major marital mishap.

Hospitality Hints

❖ Know that your manager depends on you to be there in the rare event you're called in to work unexpectedly.

❖ Every day holds positive experiences. A positive attitude will help you notice them.

❖ Look for humor in your day. You will find it.

❖ Be careful not to jump to conclusions when someone says something to you that seems a little odd at first. Ask questions to clarify their intent.

4

He Isn't Just Sleeping

The hotel operator and the security team did all they could to help the guest. Protocol ensured that only the few involved knew what was taking place. Marie will never forget the room number or her general manager's response.

The call came as our PBX switchboard operators, Marie and Dorothy, settled back to catch their breath from the morning rush. However, the moment didn't last long.

Marie picked up the phone to answer another call.

"I need someone to check on my husband. He's a guest in your hotel and has not answered his phone all morning."

"Yes, of course, ma'am. We are happy to do that for you." Marie could hear the concern in the caller's voice.

After twenty-five years at our hotel, Marie was very familiar with this type of request, though it usually came from a meeting coordinator checking on a late attendee.

"May I have your husband's name?"

"John Howard. He's in room 1928."

Marie checked her computer to confirm the room number.

"We talk every morning when he travels. It isn't like him to not answer."

"I understand, ma'am. I'll have our security officer go up to his room right away."

She placed Mrs. Howard on hold, then followed hotel procedure and called the room herself before she dispatched security. After no answer, Marie immediately dispatched Nick, the security officer.

Like Marie, Nick was familiar with this type of call. Typically, the guest is in the shower or still in bed asleep.

The tall security officer arrived at Mr. Howard's door within three minutes.

"Security," he announced as he knocked.

"Security!" He knocked louder.

Nick placed his key card against the lock, then slowly opened the door as he peered into the room.

"Mr. Howard? Security!"

Nick saw the guest lying on his bed. He inched his way over.

"Mr. Howard?"

He placed his hand on the guest's shoulder.

"Mr. Howard?" *Oh, no.*

Nick stepped back. He immediately knew something was wrong. Very wrong.

He felt for a pulse, then hurried to the phone.

"911. What's your emergency?"

"This is security officer Nick Hayes. We have a middle-aged male guest who is unresponsive."

Nick gave the details, then hung up to call his manager. "Dave, we've got a code blue in room 1928. The guest is not responding. I need you here ASAP!"

"I'm on my way!"

Dave was to the room swiftly and out of breath. As they looked at the guest, Nick filled him in. "PBX dispatched me for a wellness check. It was too late to do CPR."

Dave checked the guest himself. He stepped back and took a deep breath. "Are the paramedics on their way?"

"Yes, sir. I instructed them to use the back entrance."

"Go ahead and meet them. I'll stay here and call Mike."

"Okay. I'll call PBX on my way down and tell them we'll need to call Mrs. Howard back shortly."

As Nick exited the room, Dave picked up the phone to call the general manager.

"Mike, I'm sorry to break this to you. We have a guest who we believe is deceased in room 1928."

"I'm on my way!"

Mike dropped the phone, then dashed out of his office. Arriving only seconds ahead of the paramedics, Dave filled the GM in.

Mike looked at the guest. "Did you perform CPR?"

"It was too late."

Nick showed the paramedics into the room. It took only a few minutes for them to report back to the GM. "Our assessment tells us he passed a few hours ago." They confirmed the worst.

Mike thanked them, then instructed, "Dave, you wrap things up with the paramedics. Nick, you post at the guest's door. Let no one in the room until the police and medical examiner arrive." He paused. "I'm going to call his wife."

Mike stepped out into the hall and shut the door behind him.

How on earth do I tell this woman her husband has passed away? He shook his head, then walked slowly toward his office. Back at his desk, he took a deep breath before picking up the phone.

"Hotel operator, this is Marie."

"Marie, this is Mike Harris. I will be down to talk to you about Mr. Howard shortly. For now, may I get his wife's phone number?"

She gave him the number, then hung up.

Mike took a deep breath as he dialed Mrs. Howard's number.

"Hello?"

"Mrs. Howard, this is Mike Harris. I'm the general manager at the hotel."

"Yes. Hello, Mike."

He heard the concern in her voice.

He gently broke the news, "Mrs. Howard, I know you have been waiting for this call anxiously, and I'm sorry to have to let you know we found your husband in his room unresponsive. The paramedics were unable to revive him."

"Oh, no," she cried.

He closed his eyes and paused. "I am so sorry."

Mike took his time as he finished the tough conversation and made sure Mrs. Howard was okay.

After a moment to gather himself, he took a deep breath and stood to go speak to the PBX operators. Upon entering their office, he turned a chair around and sat down. They pivoted to face him.

"Marie and Dorothy, I want you both to know you did a good job handling the situation. Mr. Howard was lying on his bed in his nightclothes. We believe he passed in his sleep."

Their countenance fell as they listened to the unbelievable report.

He assured them, "There is nothing you or any one of us could have done to have changed the situation."

Mike spent thirty minutes with the operators answering their questions and reassuring them. He commended them for following hotel protocol with urgent care. The ladies thanked Mike for taking the time to talk to them.

It was a sad day at the hotel, but the team had jobs to do so they got back to work. They were thankful that tomorrow would be a new day.

Hospitality Hints

❖ Know your procedures regarding medical emergencies.

❖ Train all managers in CPR.

❖ Use care and professionalism in all circumstances.

❖ Acknowledge the team members who handle an emergency. Doing so will reinforce a job well done and boost morale.

5

A Lotta Loot

There is a good reason most guests pay for travel with a credit card, not cash. Here we discover how two lucky guests learned that lesson amid panic.

A Small Fortune

On **the day of Mr.** Howel's departure, his in-house meeting ran late. He hurried to his room with no time to spare, packed his bags, and arrived downstairs just in time for the 4:30 p.m. shuttle. After a fifteen-minute ride to the airport, he thanked the driver and exited the vehicle. During his short walk to baggage claim, it hit him.

I left a bag at the hotel!

He grimaced at the thought of being delayed for his flight.

It was about that time that Alice, our housekeeping manager, received a call on her radio from Kerry Ann, one of her team members.

"Ms. Alice, I think you should come up here. A guest left something very valuable in his room."

Alice went straight up to meet Kerry Ann. She was stunned as she looked inside the small black bag on the desk. "Oh, someone's going to be looking for this."

Alice picked up the bag and thanked Kerry Ann for calling her. The housekeeper nodded and resumed cleaning the room.

As Alice walked down the hallway, she radioed Doug, our security officer, asking that he meet in her office. Doug was at her office door when she arrived. The two sat in disbelief as they counted nine thousand dollars in cash.

Mystified, Alice looked at Doug. "Can you believe this?"

"It's very unusual." Doug shook his head.

"The guest is with a group, so there's no reason for concern." Alice shrugged her shoulders, then picked up the phone to call the hotel operator.

"Marie, if you receive a call from someone who left a black bag in their room, transfer the call to Doug or me." Alice hung up the phone.

Doug returned to his office. He wasted no time before placing the bag in his safe.

Fewer than five minutes later, Marie received the expected call.

"My name is Thomas Howel. Your driver just dropped me off at the airport, and I left a very important bag in my room." His tone was urgent but calm.

"Oh, yes, Mr. Howel. We've been expecting your call. I'll connect you with our security officer, Doug."

"No, I just need someone to get my bag and bring it to me as quickly as possible, so I don't miss my flight."

She assured Mr. Howel that Doug was waiting to speak to him, ready to help. She connected the call.

Doug set Mr. Howell at ease by letting him know he had the bag. The two agreed to meet at the airport in fifteen minutes. Thanks to the hotel shuttle driver, Doug arrived at the airport at the arranged time. After a quick ID check, he handed the guest his bag.

With only a glance in the bag, a "Thank you," and a handshake, Mr. Howel turned quickly to catch his flight.

Doug thought it odd that the guest seemed more concerned about missing his flight than recovering his small fortune. When he returned to the hotel, he walked to the PBX office to report to Marie. "Mission accomplished." He lowered his voice. "You wouldn't believe what was in that bag."

"What was it?"

He could see he had her attention. "Thousands of dollars."

"Oh, my. Why would someone travel with that much money?"

Doug nodded. His raised eyebrows and shrugged shoulders punctuated his story.

"Well, he's just lucky we got it back to him," Marie continued. "Did he give you a reward?"

Doug shook his head. "Nope."

They both laughed then returned to work.

Note: Kerry Ann received an employee of the year award for honesty and integrity.

A Loaded Wallet

The hotel was active with guests in-house for meetings. Everyone seemed to be in a hurry, including Jack, our food and beverage director. As he stepped off the stairs near the meeting rooms, he noticed a man's wallet on the floor. He picked it up and opened it as he walked inside the business center.

He noticed the ID, then gasped at the amount of cash inside. Jack turned to the business center clerk. "Would you call security and ask Doug to come see me?"

Doug, our security officer, arrived promptly.

"Hey Doug, look what I found on the floor." Jack opened the wallet. "Take a look at this."

Doug's eyes grew big as he looked inside. They both sat down at the nearby desk to take inventory of the contents.

Doug picked up the phone to call the operator. "Marie, can you tell me if a Mike Harris is a registered guest?"

Marie confirmed that Mike Harris was indeed registered. She gave Doug his cell phone number. Doug immediately made the call but was disappointed when there was no answer. He left a message.

At lunchtime, Mr. Harris approached the front desk and asked to speak to security about his lost wallet. Doug met the guest and invited him to step into the office to confirm the wallet's contents.

"Looks like it's all here." Mr. Harris let out a big breath. "Thank you." He shook Doug's hand and turned to go back to his meeting.

Doug stepped back to the PBX office to report the wallet was returned to the guest.

"Ok, thank you, Doug." Marie, the operator, joked. "Did you get a reward?"

"Nope."

Hospitality Hints

❖ Hire honest, trustworthy people. Check references and do a background check.

❖ Always do what is right, whether others are watching or not.

❖ Don't judge the worth of a guest by their appearance. Remember, the guest in front of you—regardless of their image or impression—may be a person of significant influence or wealth.

❖ Offer the same level of excellent hospitality to everyone.

❖ If you find a lost item, turn it in to lost and found without delay. It's the right thing to do.

For the Guest

❖ If you lose something and it's returned fully intact, consider rewarding the finder.

6

A Hot Topic

In the stillness of their shift, the night audit team was surprised by an unwelcome visitor. The situation could easily have gotten out of hand had it not been for the team's quick action and united effort.

The night supervisor tipped her nose in the air. *Is that smoke I smell?* She peered out into the lobby from behind the front desk. The lobby bar was closed, and guests were tucked away in their rooms. The area was quiet, a stillness only known to night auditors. Soft, ambient music played in the background as the night sky blanketed the hotel.

Darlene looked around, then stepped inside the office door behind the front desk. "Do you smell that?" she asked Tim, the manager.

"Do I smell what?" He sniffed.

"Oh, yes, I do." Tim rose from his chair and walked out into the middle of the lobby. Darlene followed.

"It's stronger right here."

Darlene walked past Tim toward the entrance. She froze. "Smoke is coming from the front door!"

"Call security!" Tim instructed as he ran past her toward the door.

Darlene ran back to the desk and picked up the phone.

Tim stepped outside to find smoke and flames shooting out of the top of the valet desk. He looked back and saw Craig, the security officer running toward him with a fire extinguisher.

"Stand back!" Craig shouted.

Darlene and Tim backed away.

Craig tested the metal door handles on the desk, then flung them open. He leaned back as the smoke billowed out toward him. He stepped in closer, pointed the extinguisher, and pulled the trigger.

The fire was out.

They all released a sigh of relief.

"What happened?" Craig stepped back with the fire extinguisher still in hand.

"I don't know. Darlene said she smelled smoke, and this is what we found." Tim motioned to the desk.

Craig ran his hand over his face. "You two go back inside. Just leave the desk. I'll take care of it. But first, I'm going to my office to review the video cameras."

Tim and Darlene returned to the front desk.

Downstairs in the security office, Craig reviewed the night's videos. It took some time, but the video footage doesn't lie. Mystery solved.

"Last call!" Marco, the bartender, announced as he wiped down the countertop in front of the slim, dark-haired man who finished the last drop of his glass of whiskey.

"Come on. Just one more?" Mr. Thomas slurred as he pleaded with the bartender.

"I'm sorry. We have to close at midnight." Marco lifted his shoulder and nodded.

"Where else can I go around here for a drink?"

Marco knew that was the last thing the guest needed. "Perhaps there's something good on TV in your room."

"I'll call a cab. They'll know." Mr. Thomas scowled. "You got a match?"

Marco handed him a box of matches.

The guest managed his way off the barstool and stumbled toward the door. He navigated his way into the lobby, where he called a cab. After returning his cell phone to his pocket, he walked toward the front door, stepped into the warm night air, and lit a cigarette. He inhaled a long drag and leaned on the tall valet desk while he waited. As the minutes passed, he lit another cigarette. He looked down and noticed the hole in the top of the desk. This time, instead of flicking the match on the brick drive, he tossed it in the opening on the desk.

"Huh. Two points."

He backed up, then lit another match and attempted to sink another "match point." Missed. He inched closer, struck another match, and tossed it.

"Bull's-eye!"

He looked up to glaring headlights pointed straight at him. His taxi pulled into the drive and stopped. He got in, pulled the door shut, and they drove away.

"That son-of-a-gun!" Craig yelled at the monitor. "He caught the desk on fire with matches he got from the bar!"

Craig marched up to the front desk to inform the night team. "A guest caught the desk on fire with our own matches! He made it his personal ashtray while he waited for a cab."

Tim and Darlene stood speechless.

"Tim, come with me and see if you can identify this joker on the video." The men turned toward the security office. Darlene stayed at the front desk.

Tim leaned in close to the monitor as he tried to identify the guest. "I have no idea who that is." He stepped back and looked at Craig.

"Well, keep an extra close eye on the front door and let me know the minute you see him." Craig insisted.

"We'll call you immediately if he returns," Tim assured before leaving the office.

All three kept a close watch for the rest of the night, but the guest was never seen again.

The next morning as I walked in the front door, I noticed the valet desk was gone. Where's the desk?" I asked the bellman.

"It went up in flames last night."

"What?"

"Yeah. A guest tried to see how many lit matches he could flick into the hole."

I smirked. "Looks like he made at least one."

Hospitality Hints

- ❖ Always investigate an unusual smell.

- ❖ If you witness a fire, handle it according to your hotel's procedures.

- ❖ Know where your fire extinguishers are stored.

- ❖ Always follow your local alcoholic beverage commission rules and regulations. Be on the alert for your guests' and hotel's safety.

7

Duck and Run

Even while on a much-needed break, accessibility to a manager is essential to the daily operation. Empowerment enables a team to handle business while a manager is away. But what if the unexpected happens?

Our spacious lobby was active, humming with guests just released from eight hours of on-property meetings. Most were on their way to the bar or headed to their guestroom.

It was my turn for evening lobby manager duty, or as some call it, *lobby lizard* duty. Though most dread it, I typically enjoy the hour spent answering guests' questions and giving directions. To me, it's like an invitation to a social event. It's especially festive when a banquet or wedding reception is on the books.

As I stepped out from behind the front desk and surveyed the lobby, I observed Wallace, the concierge, behind his desk and engaged in conversation with a guest. Jimmy, the doorman, managed valet parking on the front drive, with cars lined up bumper-to-bumper.

Halfway into my shift, I was excited to see Rob and Regina Macey, frequent guests and now personal friends of mine. As they walked in the front door, we made eye contact. Regina's smile and radiant personality lit up the lobby. "Hi, Kim!" She excitedly walked toward me, extending her arms.

After chatting and catching up, the Maceys and their bellman were off to their room.

As the driver stood in the center of the lobby, he maintained tradition and rang three notes on the deep-toned mini xylophone. He announced, "Five o'clock airport shuttle now departing!" It never fails to silence the lobby. The driver returned the chime to its place on the concierge desk, then walked out the door to his vehicle.

That chime also means my lobby shift is over, and it's time for dinner.

I informed the front desk team I would be downstairs in the cafeteria. "I have my radio if you need to reach me."

After going through the salad bar, I took the nearest seat with my dinner tray, relieved to be off my feet.

Little did I know what was unfolding upstairs.

"Call 911!"

Wallace, the concierge, looked up to see Jimmy run inside through the front door, bent over at the waist.

Breathless, Jimmy ducked behind Wallace's desk. "Call 911!"

Wallace reached for his phone. "What happened?!"

"A man at the end of the drive just robbed someone, and then he pointed the gun at me!"

A few bites into my salad, I received a call from a frantic desk agent requesting my presence. I put down my fork, picked up my radio, and hurried upstairs. On my way, I called Nick in security. He said he was on his way to the lobby.

On arrival and out of breath from climbing the stairs, Nick and I hurried to Jimmy's side.

I spoke first. "What happened?"

"I don't know. I walked out to help a guest. I looked up and saw a car skid in behind another car at the end of the drive. Two men wearing black ski masks jumped out and hit one of the two men from the other car on the head with a gun. The gunmen grabbed two suitcases from the other guy, then one of them pointed the gun at me. That's when I ran inside."

Nick and Jimmy peered out the front door.

"They're gone now." Jimmy saw only the victims.

Nick exited. Two police cars blazed up to the front drive as Nick ran the few yards to the scene. I remained in the lobby. The flashing lights didn't faze guests. They were oblivious to the fact an armed robbery had just taken place.

The officers stepped cautiously out of their vehicles and walked over to the two men near the car with the trunk open—one man stood, and the other sat on the grass, holding his head.

One officer bent down to talk to the injured man, then spoke into the microphone attached to his vest. "We need an ambulance. Head wound. Forty-year-old male."

The other officer spoke to the man standing. "What happened here?"

"We just drove in from the airport and were robbed." He motioned toward his trunk. "And they hit my business partner over the head."

While the police took statements, I sent Wallace out to manage the front drive.

Jimmy peeked out the glass door, then walked back toward me. "The police are walking this way."

The officers approached us and turned to Jimmy. After getting his statement, they summarized the incident for me. "The two men said they are in town from Las Vegas for a jewelry convention. The thieves followed them from the airport, pulled up behind them, and stole two suitcases that contained their merchandise. I think your security officer will tell you the guests wish to cancel their reservations."

After I thanked the officers, they went on their way.

I turned to Nick, who had just walked in the door, "Thank you, Nick, for your quick response and your assistance. And thank you, Jimmy, for your quick thinking and getting out of danger's way. Why don't you call it a day?"

Jimmy sighed in relief, then went to clock out. Nick headed downstairs to write his security report.

I walked to my desk to call our general manager. He picked up on the third ring.

"Mr. Hardy, I'm sorry to bother you at home, but we've had an incident at the hotel . . ."

◆ ◆ ◆

The two victims tried to sue the hotel for the incident, but the case never went to court. After two months of investigation, the detectives had enough information to conclude the men had staged the event.

Case closed.

Hospitality Hints

* Carry your phone or two-way radio with you at all times.

* Train your team to be alert to their surroundings and how to do that appropriately.

* Be compassionate to employees. Stress-filled experiences such as this can create the need for understanding or empathy.

* Help where you are needed. If you are unsure what is needed, ask, "How can I help?"

8

Phone Photos, Overexposed

The hotel was in peak season—the front desk fully staffed. With everything running smoothly, my world was right. Little did I know the front desk operation was about to be turned upside down.

Kim, I'm going to have to quit!" My assistant manager, Cathy, cried into the receiver.

"What's wrong, Cathy?" Concerned, I leaned in to listen closely.

"Something terrible has happened." She continued to cry.

I paused to give her time to compose herself. "Cathy, what happened?"

The story began.

"Gavin and I worked together yesterday. When I went to dinner, I forgot to take my cell phone. I left it at my desk." Her crying slowed a bit. "You remember when you and I ate together in the cafeteria the other day? I took a picture of my food and sent it to my husband."

"Yes, I remember."

"Well, I have other pictures on my phone, Kim. *Personal* pictures."

"Okay," I replied gently.

"Gavin found my phone, and he copied my pictures to his phone. Then he showed all the guys at the hotel. The bellman, security, everyone!"

Cathy? You? The most seemingly innocent, wholesome team member I have? It took a minute for what she said to sink in.

40

"Kim, I am so sorry, but I just can't come back to work knowing what they've all seen."

I thought about asking her to reconsider her decision to allow me time to handle the situation. But even I didn't see a way for her to return.

I apologized that the incident happened and assured Cathy I would investigate and address the issue immediately.

I hung up and called our HR director, Angela. I shared the information Cathy described.

"You've got to be kidding me. Gavin did what? And it was *Cathy's* pictures?" Angela was equally surprised, and I could tell she wasn't happy.

"I know. I couldn't believe it either. I'll talk to Gavin when he arrives for work this afternoon. I'll let you know what he says."

When Gavin arrived, I asked him to meet with me in my office.

He sat in front of my desk, and I opened the conversation.

"Gavin, I received a call from Cathy today. She said you stole pictures of her from her phone, then showed multiple employees. Is that true?"

His blank expression never changed.

"Pictures? No. I don't know anything about pictures." His manner was calm, and as usual, his words were few.

I knew Gavin wasn't perfect, but I thought I could trust him regarding matters of integrity. Otherwise, I would not have promoted him—or hired him in the first place.

"You're telling me you know nothing about this?" I paused.

He shook his head. "No. I know nothing about it. It wasn't me." He maintained his expressionless stance.

Dissatisfied with Gavin's unconcerned response, I thanked him and dismissed him to return to the front desk. Unfortunately, as a new supervisor, Gavin had not yet earned my trust. And this was not helping his case.

I picked up the phone and called Angela.

"I spoke to Gavin, but he denied knowing about Cathy's pictures."

Angela sighed. "So, it's her word against his."

"Yes. But I believe Cathy. So, how can we prove it?"

Angela was silent for a moment. "Give me a day or two."

By the end of the next day, Angela had evidence that Gavin was indeed the guilty party. Shane, a bellman, who later went on to become a police officer, told her everything. His statement matched Cathy's exactly.

The next day, seated in front of Angela's desk, I called Gavin. "Gavin, can you come to see me in Angela's office, please?"

As he walked into the room, I stood from my chair and closed the door.

"Have a seat," Angela instructed him.

I took my seat next to Gavin.

Angela leaned in as she sat at her desk. Then she got right to business.

"Gavin, I was informed that you have pictures of Cathy on your phone. Pictures she didn't authorize you to have."

Gavin shook his head. "I don't have any pictures on my phone."

"Cathy said she left her phone on her desk while on break two nights ago, and you accessed her photos, transferred them to your phone, then shared them with other employees."

"It wasn't me." Gavin continued to play innocent.

"It is best for you to tell me the truth, Gavin. I have a statement from a witness to what you did."

Gavin went silent.

After a few seconds, he spoke.

"Okay, it was me."

Angela heard what she was waiting for, and I was relieved to hear the truth.

"Gavin, I will remind you that in your orientation, you were told that we have a zero-tolerance for sexual harassment. Because of what you did, your employment is terminated, effective immediately. I need the key to your bank and your name tag."

I don't think that was the response he expected to his confession.

Gavin sighed. "Okay."

I turned to Gavin. "Do you have any personal belongings at the front desk?"

"No. I don't." He handed his key and name tag to Angela.

"You can pick up your final check tomorrow," Angela instructed as Gavin stood.

I walked him out of the office. Then a security officer escorted him out of the building, a standard practice for all employees who are terminated involuntarily.

I walked back into the HR office. "Good job, Angela."

"I'm just glad he confessed sooner than later." She shook her head.

"I'm sorry this happened to Cathy. And I'm sorry to see her go. She was a good manager."

"Yes. She was."

Angela and I resumed our workday. I went to my office and called Cathy. I thanked her for being an outstanding manager and coming forward with the information about Gavin's actions. I let her know he confessed, and HR had terminated his employment. Cathy thanked me for calling her. We both expressed disappointment in the situation. Before the conversation ended, she asked if I would write her a recommendation letter.

"Yes, of course. I'm happy to. You were an outstanding manager, Cathy, and I'm sorry to see you go. Your new employer will be fortunate to have you on their team."

Cathy thanked me for everything.

After hanging up the phone, I got busy revising the weekly schedule and processing the paperwork for the sudden open positions. All of us at the front desk worked a little harder for a few weeks while I interviewed new applicants, but it was a small price to pay to ensure Cathy received justice and Gavin learned there are consequences to his actions.

I hoped they learned valuable lessons, and I wished them both the best.

Hospitality Hints

- ❖ Implement and consistently enforce a zero-tolerance sexual harassment policy at your hotel. Inform and train all team members in orientation and provide a refresher course annually.

- ❖ Inform all team members of what to expect.

- ❖ Assure your team that they can talk to you any time.

- ❖ If a team member reports an issue to you, take it seriously and handle it according to your hotel's procedures.

- ❖ Password protect your phone and suggest others do as well.

9

Fright Fest

The sales team gave the managers an overview of the large group arriving the coming weekend. No matter how prepared our team was, we never could have predicted how frightfully unique this group would be.

One of the most memorable moments from this particular weekend was when I looked up from my computer at the front desk to see a man dressed as a pig on roller skates. He held a drink in each hand. The pig-man skated out of the lobby bar toward the conference center as though his appearance was not unusual. Well, that day, his appearance *wasn't* unusual. Why? Because the hotel was invaded by Zombie Fest the previous day. So, Mr. Scary Pig Man fit right in.

Three hundred actors and enthusiasts came together to meet about all things zombie. There were even a few big-name celebrities included in the group for autographs. They were well known for their starring roles in macabre films.

Check-in day was as typical as it could be. However, the first evening gave us a glimpse of what to expect for the next three days. The actors applied elaborate zombie makeup, donned full costumes, and then roamed the hotel all night—inside and out.

The hotel staff was wide-eyed from strange sights all weekend long. I'm certain the group would consider it a compliment.

Our VIP lounge concierge—who never calls me—dialed my number the first night. "Kim, what is going on? I have monsters in my lounge." I could hear disbelief and puzzlement in her voice.

Somehow, her direct manager had forgotten to fill her in on what to expect from our unusual group of guests.

Later that same night, our security officer handled a complaint from a female zombie guest who protested the behavior of a male zombie guest with her group. As they stood at the end of the front desk, I overheard her say, "I don't know why he bit me. Zombies aren't supposed to bite each other. They only bite *real* people."

Day two was featured as the main day of the convention. The actors and celebrities signed autographs for the group in the main convention hall at the rear of the hotel.

Meanwhile, at the mall two blocks away, a group of guests in full makeup and costume assembled for a "zombie walk" that was about to begin. A red truck with a large black machine gun in the bed led the procession. The monsters grunted, growled, and limped in character while a man in the bed of the truck pretended to be escaping them as the driver drove from the mall to the hotel.

As the horde dramatically approached our property, the truck pulled into the front drive. The zombies continued their grunting and growling—as zombies naturally should. Then suddenly, without warning, the man in the back of the truck started shooting blanks out of the machine gun. It was so loud that a few front desk employees hit the floor. Karl, our assistant general manager, who heard the commotion from his third-floor office, scurried down the stairs and out the front door. Thanks to him, the madness stopped within seconds.

That weekend, one non-zombie guest after another canceled their reservation when they realized what they had walked into. A lady and her six-year-old daughter made it all the way from the front door to the front desk to check in before the scene registered with her and she noticed the creatures that surrounded her. As she casually looked around, she realized this was no ordinary day at the hotel. Clearly startled, she covered her child's eyes and asked to check in as quickly as possible.

Picking up on her concern, the front desk agent explained, "We are hosting a zombie actors' convention this weekend."

Then the two dashed toward their room with the mother's hand still blocking her child's view.

I shook my head. *Poor thing. She must have had a non-refundable reservation.*

Another guest called on his cell phone. "I just pulled into your parking lot and pulled right back out. What is going on at your hotel?"

The operator explained.

The caller responded, "Go ahead and cancel my reservation."

It wasn't just the guests who were in disbelief. The employees wore looks of astonishment and overwhelm the entire weekend. But, of course, as always, we kept up and offered our usual high level of service to these most unusual looking (and acting) guests.

Though we appreciated them and the entertainment they offered all weekend long, the group's departure day couldn't have come soon enough. Our housekeeping manager, Alice, was up in arms and the most affected. The rooms were a disaster. Makeup and red dye were all over the walls, the bed linen. Everywhere.

"Kim, it's going to take forever to clean the rooms. There's no way we can get the stains out of the sheets and blankets. Even the public restrooms were destroyed."

I sympathized with Alice, as did our general manager, Scott.

In our staff meeting three days later, we talked at length about our Zombie Fest group. At the conclusion of the meeting, Scott filled us in on our plan for the future.

"The zombie group were nice people and mostly well behaved. But unfortunately, we learned the hard way that our hotel was not cut out to host this kind of group. Though we love a good challenge, damage to the property and the uneasiness of the non-group guests would prevent us from seeking out such groups in the future."

I could almost hear the collective sigh from the management team. Meeting adjourned.

Hospitality Hints

- ❖ Become aware of groups' planned events and scheduled activities and how they will affect your business, other guests, and staff.

- ❖ When a unique convention reserves the majority of your hotel, consider advising non-participating guests before their arrival. Block rooms for them on a floor separate from the group.

- ❖ Show appreciation for all types of groups. Ensure service levels are maintained.

- ❖ If hotel property is damaged by a guest or numerous guests, follow standard operating procedures.

10

The Guest Is Always Right?

What do you think? Is the guest always right? Does the guest always speak the truth? Let's take a stroll down Anomaly Lane and decide together.

M s. Kim, the guest over there"—the bellman indicated the man with a nod in his direction—"wants to speak to the manager." Jordan, the bellman, towered over me, which required him to bend down for a quick conversation. "He said the airport shuttle left without him. He wants us to take him in his own *personal* shuttle."

I've heard that before. We looked out into the lobby.

I nodded. "Thanks, Jordan. I'm happy to speak to him. Lead the way."

As we walked to the center of the large, open lobby, Jordan spoke out of the side of his mouth. "I know for sure the shuttle left right on time, Ms. Kim."

"Thank you, Jordan." *Now, let's see how the guest will plead his case.*

Jordan mumbled as he turned toward his post, "He's just makin' stuff up."

I continued and walked the few steps to the guest. "Hi there, my name is Kim." I extended my hand. "I understand you would like to take our shuttle to the airport."

The guest spoke in a matter-of-fact tone. "That's right. I was here on time." He pointed to the floor where he stood. "And your shuttle just left without me."

52

Hmmm. Not the typical outrage or impatience of a guest who indeed was here on time and is now late for his flight. I need to listen here with a grain of salt.

Carefully, I inquired, "So, you were here before three o'clock, and the shuttle left without you?"

The guest looked down. "Yes, I was right here."

So let me get this straight. Before our driver departs for the airport, he gets out of his shuttle, walks in the front door, stands in the center of the lobby, gongs a mini xylophone, then yells at the top of his lungs, "Three o'clock shuttle now departing!" And he somehow missed you?

I looked around the room in a brief pause while I mused to allow the guest to say anything else.

"May I have your name, sir?"

"My name is Ben Lions."

"Mr. Lions, excuse me a moment. I will check with dispatch to see if we have another driver available."

I walked to the transportation office to speak with the dispatcher.

"Manny, a guest missed the shuttle. Do you have another driver available?"

Manny informed me that David, the driver, was currently in the parking lot and would pull up momentarily.

I thanked Manny, then returned to the guest. "Mr. Lions, we happen to have another shuttle driver available. If you meet him on the front drive, he will take you to the airport."

The guest picked up his luggage and followed me to the door.

I motioned toward the vehicle as it approached. "This is your shuttle. Have a great day, Mr. Lions. Thank you for staying with us."

Mr. Lions thanked me and boarded the shuttle. I stood at the door as the guest departed, then I turned to walk back inside. When I was halfway through the lobby, another male guest approached me.

"Ma'am, can I talk to you for a minute?"

I turned and smiled at the guest, who seemed to come out of nowhere.

He continued. "I know that guy. I work with him. And he just lied to you. He was *not* here on time for the shuttle."

"Oh, really?" I looked at him with interest. But I instantly knew it was an opportunity to take the high road. I let the guest finish.

"That's right. Our meeting broke late, so he didn't make it on time."

Do you step out of nowhere and expose non-truths like this all the time? I have waited for this moment all of my hospitality life. And now that it's here, I want to handle it well.

"Thank you for that." I continued. "Either way, he needed to get to the airport quickly." I shrugged my shoulders and smiled. "We're happy to help him."

We both looked through the glass doors. I turned to the guest. "Thank you for the information. I appreciate it. You have a great day."

I continued my walk back to the front desk, where Jordan, the bellman, approached me again. "Ms. Kim, thank you for helping the guest, but I know he was not here on time."

I kindly reassured him, "It's okay, Jordan."

"Yeah, Ms. Kim. I guess you're right. It's okay. He just needed to get to the airport, didn't he?"

"That's right, Jordan. He just needed to get to the airport."

Hospitality Hints

❖ Always listen to the guests as if they speak the truth. Give them the benefit of the doubt.

❖ If you can give the guest what they want—within reason—give it to them.

❖ Never let pride or any other personal feelings influence your decisions.

❖ If you must say no, tell the guest what you *can* do for him.

11

The Pinball Wizard and
the Watered Loo

Hotel staff can expect plumbing malfunctions
just like we would at home. Many malfunctions.
Is your engineering department prepared?
Seconds could make the difference
between a dribble and a deluge.

Leisure groups, parties, dinners, and celebrations make our weekends come alive. The annual dance school competition is my favorite of all the groups that grace our property. As young people walk to and from classes and rehearsals, we get to see their eclectic costumes and experience their high energy. Mid-day, our security officers have to clear pathways through the sea of hungry dancers sitting cross-legged in the lobby and eating Chick-fil-A. They need every nook and cranny for practice.

I remember one competitor in the lobby who miscalculated the consecutive number of cartwheels the room could allow and crashed, legs up, into the sliding glass door. Not to worry, she and the door were both okay.

With no offense to others, my least favorite weekend group is the karate competition. Friendly people, but the aroma of bare feet mixed with sweat makes for a memorable and odorous occasion. Not to mention the sound of those sockless feet slapping across the tile floor all day long.

One summer weekend, we welcomed a unique group of another kind—pinball enthusiasts. Four hundred of them. Before their arrival, convention planners filled the grand hall with modern and vintage machines for players and enthusiasts.

One player was especially memorable, but not for his game.

"Good afternoon." I greeted the young dark-haired man as he approached the desk.

"I'm checking in for the convention."

I commented on his purple T-shirt that read Pinball Wizard. "You must be good at your game."

He cracked a smile and looked down at his shirt.

Within a few minutes, the check-in was complete. "You will find your convention on the lower level." I motioned to the left, then handed him his room key. "Your elevator is down the hall. Enjoy your stay. And please let us know if we may be of assistance."

He turned and strolled toward his room.

I moved on to greet the next guest.

Thirty minutes later, I picked up a call. "Front desk, this is Kim. How may I help you?"

"I'm downstairs by the convention. There's a water leak in the men's restroom. The handle on the toilet broke."

I recognized the voice. It was the pinball wizard.

"Oh, I'm so sorry. Thank you for reporting the leak. I'll send someone right away."

I hung up the phone and reported to Marie, our PBX switchboard supervisor. She, in turn, dispatched Alberto, our engineer.

The keys on Alberto's belt loop jingled while he walked from one side of the building to the other.

His boots squished on the soaked carpet as he approached the restroom door. He looked down. "This isn't good."

Inside, the sound of rushing water came from across the room. He quickly sloshed his way over to the stall and the suspected source of the sudden flood. As he pushed the swinging door open, he reeled at the sight of a geyser-like gush of water shooting straight up out of the flush pipe.

He jumped back, then grabbed his radio. "Lance, come in!"

"Go ahead."

"We have a broken pipe in the men's room, lower level! Shut off the valve!"

The engineering director sprang from his chair and ran down the hall. He reached the valve and cranked it off. "Did that take care of it!?"

"No. It's still on! We have a major leak. Hurry!"

Alberto tried to stop the rush of water with his hands, to no avail. He got a soaking shower instead.

Lance ran up the fire escape stairs, cranked the second valve, then ran back down to the flooded restroom. He stood panting and out of breath as water poured out of the restroom and into the meeting rooms like a tsunami.

"I shut off both valves! That should have taken care of it." Lance shook his head, then turned to Alberto and snapped his fingers. "I'll be right back." Lance splashed through the water again and ran back down the hall to check the plumbing blueprints. Alberto guarded the door against guest entry.

"There it is." He hit the paper on his desk, then took off in the direction of the third valve.

"This has to be the right one." Lance heaved the knob to the off position.

"It's off now, Lance!" Alberto's voice blared over his radio.

Lance sighed. "Okay, Alberto! Thank you."

Back in the restroom, Lance looked at Alberto. "What happened?"

"I don't know. PBX called and said a guest reported a leak."

"This is no leak, Alberto. This is a break."

Housekeeping hurried with wet vacs and carts of towels to begin the clean-up.

Furious, Lance contacted PBX to see where the call originated. Then he and Brian, our conference director, came to see me.

After filling me in, they asked if I knew who reported the break.

"Yes, I do. A young man I checked in earlier. He said it broke."

Brian huffed. "It didn't break on its own. Can you identify him?"

"Yes, I can."

Brian nodded. "Good. I'm calling the police. We're going to find this joker."

Minutes later, Brian, two police officers, and I approached the convention room door. Brian waited in the hall while I led the officers inside. The music and plinking machines blasted as we walked in.

I turned back to the officers and shouted, "I'll walk around. Do you want to follow me?"

They nodded.

I felt like an agent on a mission to find the perpetrator.

I scanned the room as I wove through the crowd. Finally, on the far side, I spotted a purple T-shirt.

That's him.

His back was toward me as he faced a machine with his arms in the play position.

I nodded to the officers. They stepped up. I walked away.

Suspect found.

The police led the young man out of the convention hall and into a private room, where they questioned his involvement in the major flood. He confessed to kicking the toilet handle out of frustration that it wouldn't flush.

Instead of pressing charges, the general manager evicted the pinball wizard and asked him not to return. Although the guest had intentionally kicked the spout, the break was unintentional.

In the end, the hotel's insurance company paid tens of thousands of dollars in damages. The managers moved current and future groups to alternate meeting spaces until the repairs were completed weeks later. At the same time, the engineering team posted signs in the back halls noting locations of the shut-off valves for quick and easy reference. There would never be a delay in locating a valve again.

Hospitality Hints

❖ Ensure the engineering team knows the locations of water shut-off valves.

❖ Be tough on issues, soft on people.

❖ Stay calm and cool under pressure. Never let them see you sweat.

❖ Even during high-traffic times at the front desk, remember to make eye contact with each guest. They will feel acknowledged, and you will have a face registered if there is anything out of the ordinary.

12

Unwelcome Guests

It's smaller than a ladybug, yet hotels consider it one of the most feared intruders. Hoteliers refuse to say its name out loud for fear of being heard by a guest. It only comes out at night, and it preys on the unsuspecting.

One of the challenges of being surrounded by vast wooded acreage is keeping native wildlife out of the hotel. When I say wildlife, I mean animals and insects. As in any hotel (or home), some will cross the battle line no matter how aggressive our efforts. I know what's coming when I see a guest walk toward the front desk with a hotel glass in hand with the white paper lid intact. There is sure to be something I do not want to see underneath that lid.

While most bugs are unpleasant and all are unwelcome, the most intrusive is the bed bug. Managers cringe upon hearing the words. We brace ourselves for a long conversation with the guest and follow up afterward.

Bed bugs, also known as BBs, are unique in how they enter the hotel. Most bugs enter by way of the door, flying in, scaling the wall, dropping down a pipe, etc. Not so with the bed bug. *Guests* are the primary importers of this little creature, which enters most often on luggage. Once inside, they have the potential to multiply and invade. Though these uninvited visitors can hide in almost any crevice, their favorite spot is bed seams. Worst of all, they creep out at night to bite the unsuspecting.

If given time to multiply, the tiny insects have the potential to shut down an entire hotel to not reopen until the little invaders are exterminated. Approval to reopen must be granted from the health department.

Of all insects, bed bugs are one of the least often reported. But beware, if a guest says something bit them during the night and they have several small red bite marks on their person, drop everything and have the room inspected immediately, following your respective hotel's procedures.

I am happy to say that thanks to preventative measures such as mattress covers, routine inspections, and extermination, the properties in which I have worked have had little to no issue with BBs. However, I have experienced other unique challenges regarding unwelcome guests—including an "invasion" of another kind.

The Invasion of 2011

In the summer of 2011, thousands of crickets invaded our property. The issue was so disturbing! From a distance, our usually light-colored parking lot appeared black as night. Horrified guests zig-zagged through the lot to avoid the crunch of bugs beneath their feet or wheels of rolling luggage.

No matter what our exterminator did, the city-wide invasion would not surrender. The attackers continued to surround our property and made their siege on the building on all sides. The battle raged with little hope of retreat by the enemy.

We had a challenge on our hands. Just one of the little creatures could keep an entire floor of guests awake at night with its chirping.

I will never forget one of our international guests who hid under his covers as he informed the bug-spray-wielding engineer, "I will not get out of this bed until you remove the bug!"

Randolf, our general manager, was livid over the attempted takeover of his hotel. I remember the grimace on his face as he banged his fist on his desk. "Crickets are not paying guests!"

While the exterminators struggled to do their part, the house-keeping manager got creative. She turned the situation into a who-can-catch-the-most-bugs contest. Every cricket was worth twenty-five cents.

Each housekeeper received a clear bag to deposit as many little black intruders as they could round up. Then, each employee turned in their bag of bugs at the end of their shift.

One day as I walked past the open housekeeping office door, I cringed and looked away when I saw Alice, the manager, holding up a clear bag as she counted the creepy little creatures inside.

The contest was a success. The housekeeping heroes caught many bugs and thus, prevented many complaints. Their efforts, combined with our exterminator and change of season, ended the plague.

Chirp, chirp.

Hospitality Hints

❖ The sight of a bug in a hotel is never acceptable to a guest.

❖ Always act as if it's the first report of a bug on your property. Never say, "Oh, that's just a . . ." You may be used to the native creature, but the guest is not.

❖ Provide your team with training on the uniqueness of a bed bug complaint and how to handle it.

❖ Get creative in the resolution.

For the Guest

❖ Use the luggage rack. Protect your bags from insects that might be on the bed or floor. You will also protect the hotel from insects that might be on your luggage.

❖ Remember, hotels are like homes. We all see a bug in our house at times, and occasionally, we'll see one in a hotel. Be kind and understanding when you report the issue.

❖ If a hotel has an evident and unusual bug issue, check out immediately.

13

When Your Reputation Speaks for You

I witnessed a violation of policy and immediately knew what I should do. When the situation took an unexpected turn, my past reputation became a factor. In times of trial and testing, how will your reputation speak for you?

As I returned my dinner tray to its place in the employee cafeteria, Robin, a security officer, walked through the entrance door. I don't think I would have noticed him had he not made an announcement.

"Hey, they've got T-bone steaks down the hall." He called over to the only other person in the cafeteria, Luis, a conference manager who sat in a nearby booth.

As if on cue, Luis stood and walked out the door toward the banquet event.

As I exited and walked past Robin, I noticed the ceramic plate with a silver cover he held in his hands. *That is no employee meal. Ours are served on pink plastic plates.*

I walked out with an uneasy clarity: Robin had violated policy, and he invited Luis to do the same.

Why would someone do such a thing? Not only are employee meals prepared by the same chef as our fine-dining restaurants, but they also only cost a dollar. Who could ask for more?

The next day during my one-on-one meeting with our assistant general manager, Karl, I mentioned he might want to appoint someone to keep an eye on the banquet situation at night. I briefly shared what I'd observed regarding two team members who'd helped themselves to food intended for a client's banquet.

He asked for the names. I gave them.

A few days later, our GM, Mr. Moore, approached me at the front desk and asked me to join him for a cup of coffee. I followed him down the hall to the coffee shop. We took our seats with drinks in hand.

"Kim, Karl told me about Robin and Luis taking steaks from an event." Mr. Moore's tone was deep and soft.

Oh, this is more serious than I thought.

I sat up a little straighter and nodded. "Yes, I did talk to Karl about it."

"When security talked to Robin, he not only denied taking a steak, but he accused *you* of taking one." Mr. Moore informed.

My brow furrowed. *He said I took a steak?* I couldn't believe it, and thankfully, I knew Mr. Moore didn't either.

"Now listen, Kim. I trust you. I know what you said is true. And I know you did *not* take a steak. But I'm not sure how to prove what Robin did. This is where I need your help. How can we prove what happened?"

I thought what I was about to say was obvious, but I said it carefully, not wanting to insult him. "Have you watched the video footage from the surveillance camera in the banquet hall?"

Mr. Moore acknowledged they had not watched the footage but agreed it was a good idea. He wrapped up our meeting and thanked me for my time.

"It's always a pleasure to talk to you, Kim. It seems like I learn something new every time we talk."

Mr. Moore was always kind and gentle. Had Robin told the truth, he would have received a written warning at most. But since he tried to cover up his actions *and* falsely accused another person, Mr. Moore wanted justice, and he was determined to get it.

About a week after our conversation, I received an update on the T-bone incident. One of the security officers informed me that Mr. Moore and the security manager watched the video footage, and it clearly showed Robin and Luis each taking a covered plate from the hot box near the event.

Because Luis admitted his involvement and it was his first policy violation, he was issued a warning.

Robin was terminated, not only for policy violation but for dishonesty and making a false accusation.

No one knew that Robin had also stolen a diamond ring from the safe just hours before his termination. Management didn't discover it until several days after his departure.

Soon after the case was closed, Mr. Moore stopped by the front desk. "Thank you for your help, Kim. Good job. Now, if we'd only had a surveillance camera on the safe that held the diamond ring."

"Is that in the works, Mr. Moore?"

His eyes squinted as he smiled. "We had it installed yesterday."

Hospitality Hints

- ❖ Keep your eyes open and stay alert.

- ❖ Report suspicious behavior.

- ❖ No matter what anyone else does, you do what is right.

- ❖ Build a good reputation. It will speak for you.

14

Midnight Meet-up
in the Stairwell

What happens when you mix problems with intoxicated guests with room key issues and broken elevators? Our night audit team of two found out firsthand.

After two hours in the lobby bar, Mr. Blackwell decided to call it a night. He tossed two twenties onto the counter to pay for his drinks, then slid off the barstool. He focused on his balance as he walked toward the door. The unsteady man paused in the lobby, unable to find a room key in his pockets. Then he changed direction, aiming for the front desk to ask for another.

The front desk agent, Annie, checked his required identification, then handed him a new key. "Here you are, Mr. Blackwell. You have a good night."

He thanked her, and turned to go to his room.

As Annie watched him walk away, she was relieved to see him walk past the bar and continue toward his guestroom tower.

Mr. Blackwell caught his reflection in the mirror on the wall as he stepped off the elevator and stumbled toward his room.

Just a little further, then I will fall into bed.

He steadied his hand as he placed his key against the door lock. Nothing happened.

He tried again—still no green light.

Mr. Blackwell's patience (and perhaps his coordination) was beginning to fail him. He tried once more and pressed fervently on the door handle. "Oh, come on."

He pivoted and walked heavy-footed back toward the elevator. "Unbelievable."

He pressed the down button to return to the first floor, then leaned against the wall.

After what he thought to be a longer than usual wait, he looked up and noticed the floor indicator screen was blank. He punched the elevator button repeatedly.

"Now, the elevator doesn't work? Unbelievable."

Infuriated, he threw his fist into the middle of the mirror on the wall. The glass shattered. He held his bleeding hand as he turned back around to take one last look at the elevator doors. They remained shut in still silence, unwilling to cooperate.

He ripped off his shirt and wrapped it around his hand, then headed toward the bright red exit sign. He entered the stairwell and began his descent.

Mr. Blackwell wasn't the only one who had elevator trouble. Two floors below, after waiting for the missing elevator herself, Mrs. Harvey was also in the stairwell.

"The elevators don't work, John," she said to her husband on the other end of her cell phone. "I'm walking down the stairwell marked "emergency exit.""

"Ok. I'll stay on the phone with you honey. Be careful."

Mr. Blackwell continued to huff loudly as his boots pounded the metal stairs.

Mrs. Harvey heard the footsteps. She tensed and whispered loudly into the phone, "John, I think there's someone in here with me."

She rushed down to the next-floor landing. The stranger's foot-steps grew louder. She tried the door handle. It wouldn't budge. She looked up and gasped at the sign on the wall.

NO RE-ENTRY

"The door won't open, John!"

She whirled around and looked up at the shirtless stranger de-scending toward her. Frightened, she dashed down the stairs again.

"John, someone's following me, and he doesn't have any clothes on! I can't get out of the stairwell!"

"*What?* Someone's following you—with no clothes on? I'm going to contact the front desk! I'll call you right back." John hung up and called the hotel.

Darlene, the second night auditor, answered the phone.

"Darlene, my wife is stuck in your stairwell, and a naked man is chasing her! You need to get her out of there right now."

After Darlene clarified what she heard, she asked, "What tower, sir?"

He didn't know.

"What is your wife's name?"

"It's Sarah Harvey."

After a quick search on the computer, with phone still in hand, Darlene picked up the two-way radio with the other hand and dis-patched James, the overnight security officer. Darlene was used to handling middle-of-the-night issues involving drunk people. She had a sense of urgency but suspected this was not as serious as it sounded.

"James, we have a lady stuck in the east tower stairwell who says a naked man is chasing her. After you handle that, would you see if the elevators are down again?"

James acknowledged and headed toward the room tower stairwell.

Darlene put the phone back to her ear. "Mr. Harvey, our security officer, is on his way to help your wife now."

James ran from his office to the first-floor stairwell. As he approached the door, the two guests walked out simultaneously.

"Are you okay, ma'am?" James asked.

"Hold on, honey. I'm out now," Mrs. Harvey took the phone from her ear.

"Yes. I'm okay. I thought I was being chased, but this man had elevator trouble too. You need to have them fixed. This is unacceptable." She tipped her nose as she walked off to return to her event.

Mr. Blackwell spoke up. "What kind of hotel is this?" he demanded. "My key doesn't work and I had to walk down eight flights of stairs."

James apologized. "We're resetting the elevators right now. The front desk can help you with your key." James offered assistance for Mr. Blackwell's hand, but he declined.

Annie, the same front desk agent who'd helped him earlier, noticed the shirtless man as he walked toward her from the east tower. Her coworker, Darlene, had already briefed her about the elevator and key issues.

"Mr. Blackwell, I'm so sorry about the elevator. We're resetting them now." Annie spoke before he did. She didn't dare question his appearance or the injured hand.

"Here is your new key. I will have James meet you at your door to be sure it works this time." Annie wished the tired, disgruntled guest a good night.

When the coast was clear, Darlene stuck her head out the office door to the front desk. "Well, that was interesting."

"Yes. I know. And it's only eleven o'clock."

Hospitality Hints

❖ An apology goes a long way.

❖ Stay calm and ask clear, concise questions during an emergency. Your calm will help others to be calm.

❖ Reassure the guest that the issue is being addressed. Provide the guest an update on the progress when appropriate.

❖ Stay professional in all circumstances.

15

Moments of Truth

In the hospitality industry, just like any other, professionals will encounter temptations and tests. They can count on it. How do they know they're ready? What will they do in the moment of truth?

Two Thousand Pennies

get excited when I see a penny on the ground. Imagine my delight when I found a twenty-dollar bill.

As I walked by the ATM in our lobby, I thought it strange to see money in the dispenser tray with no one around. I stepped up to the machine and removed the twenty-dollar bill. I looked around again, expecting someone to come out from nowhere to tell me it was theirs. Since no one came running toward me, I followed procedure and turned the money over to the security department. Don, the morning officer, placed it in the safe where the hotel stores valuables. There it would stay for thirty days. If unclaimed, the money would be returned to the finder. Me!

Guests almost never call for lost cash unless it's regarding thousands of dollars, which *has* happened, as you read in the chapter titled, "A Lotta Loot."

I fully expected to be twenty dollars richer at the end of thirty days. And I was not disappointed.

Since my lucky find, I made it a point to glance at the ATM tray every time I walked by. I've hit the jackpot about once a month.

One day when I was halfway down the lobby stairs, I spotted money in the ATM tray again. It was as if rocket fuel filled my black pumps. I blasted off and was in front of the ATM before anyone else noticed it.

Forty dollars!

I went through the same procedural routine and gave our security officer the two twenties, but something seemed different this time. I had found a twenty just last week. The timing and the amount of money told me this could be a test.

Our security director, Mark, knew the exact time I would walk downstairs from my weekly meeting. It would be just like him to place two twenties in the machine to see if I would turn in a more considerable amount.

Was it a test? To this day, I don't know.

But thirty days later, I was forty dollars richer.

Lifted Lawn Equipment

After his induction, Dan Moore, our new general manager, took the time to evaluate the productivity and management of each department. His goal was to limit waste, overtime, repetitive and non-productive processes, and the like.

One day, I overheard Dan ask another manager about the credentials and job duties of Ben, our landscaping manager. Ben was responsible for the hotel's landscaping crew, and for more than twenty years, he'd done outstanding work. He and his crew did an excellent job maintaining our lush green lawn and flower gardens.

One of the general manager's important responsibilities was a quarterly assessment of the landscaping department, which included a review of invoices and an inventory of the utility shed.

During his first assessment, he discovered that two new pieces of lawn equipment appeared to be missing, according to recent invoices. Dan requested assistance from the security manager.

The manager confirmed the equipment was missing and not misplaced or stored elsewhere. Now it was time to request assistance from our HR director, Angela. She called Ben into her office. Ben's manager, Lance, sat in front of Angela's desk.

Angela addressed the issue of missing equipment with Ben. Lance remained silent.

Ben shifted in his seat. "Everything should be in the shed," he insisted.

"Ben, we took inventory of the equipment in the shed and the engineering shop. The equipment you just purchased is not on property." Angela replied.

"Well, I might have it at home. But I was given permission to use it. Lance said I could use the equipment for my side job." Ben sounded defensive.

Angela turned her attention to Lance. "Lance, tell me about your conversation with Ben regarding hotel equipment."

Lance looked at Ben. "Ben, I said you could use the *old* equipment after it was replaced with new equipment. You took the *new* equipment."

Angela spoke. "Ben, what you did is theft of hotel property." Her voice softened. "I'm sorry, but we have to let you go."

Ben's termination surprised us all. It was a reminder to keep the line between our personal and professional lives very clear regarding relationships, hotel property, and services.

My Found Item Is Lost

Brit, our evening security officer, helped manage lost-and-found items and inquiries for his department. He was a friendly man. Always cheerful.

When Brit received a call about a lost item, he would search the lost-and-found log. Then if found, he would place the item in the mail.

After Brit's first anniversary, Mark, the security manager, started receiving numerous complaints from guests who said they had not received their items in the mail. Each claimed they previously spoke to someone who said the article had been found and they would receive it within a week. So, Mark, the investigator, jumped into action.

Upon conclusion of his investigation, Mark determined that Brit never mailed the lost items. He took them home instead.

Brit's short-term dishonest gain cost him his long-term honest employment.

Hospitality Hints

❖ Know and follow hotel policies and procedures.

❖ Be resolved to always do what is right.

❖ Every right decision leads to growth and maturity.

❖ During new hire training, provide your team with clear communication regarding the consequences of policy violations.

❖ Help your team understand that your conversations will always be truthful and straightforward, and you expect the same from them.

❖ Always expect the best from your team. When they make the right choice, your acknowledgment may help them make it their consistent practice.

16

Double Trouble

When the team loses track of rooms inventory and guests come up short on comfort, someone must pay. Our scramble to keep guests happy, whatever the cost, could have been prevented had I paid attention.

Our staff meeting included important information our front desk team needed for an upcoming event, so I stopped by to bring them up to speed.

"A large group arrives in one week. They have contracted the majority of our double rooms. Watch the inventory daily to ensure we don't overbook."

I answered a few questions and asked them to follow up with me on any additional concerns or issues before I hurried back to my desk.

As a new manager, my schedule was incredibly busy, and I let the week get away from me. I didn't follow up with the staff or watch the numbers myself. Boy, do I wish I had.

I arrived mid-morning on the day of the major lingerie company's big event. I would cover the mid shift and oversee their check-in, which began at 10:00 a.m. and would finish before their 7:00 p.m. banquet event. Four hundred district managers from all over the country were flying in to be pampered and awarded for their accomplishments.

As usual, I checked in with the team first thing. I interrupted Tina, the front desk supervisor, from what appeared to be intense work. "How is the day?" I knew it would be important to monitor occupancy and our double-room inventory.

Tina looked up from her computer. "I'm trying to balance our room types. It looks like we're short on double rooms for today's arrivals."

"What do you mean we're short on double rooms?" I was immediately concerned. "We were supposed to protect them for the group arriving today."

My tone prompted her to explain. "We have two-hundred check-ins left, and we're forty double rooms short. Over the past two days the team must have changed king room reservations to doubles for early check-ins that didn't want to wait for their king rooms to be cleaned."

Oh, no. This is not good. I must move fast!

I sped to my desk and called our housekeeping director. "Alice, how many rollaway beds do we have?"

"Um, let me see." She said in her thick southern drawl. "Fifteen."

"Alice, we are short *forty double rooms* for today's group arrivals. The entire group will check in by 7:00 p.m."

"Forty?! Oh, my goodness." Alice jumped into action. "Let me get on the phone with our rental company. I'll call you back."

I waited to break the news to our assistant general manager, Karl, until I knew our backup plan was secured.

Alice called back within ten minutes. "They've got 'em, but it's going to cost us $3,000."

Oh, dear. I sank inside. *This is really not good.*

We had no other option. "Get them here ASAP, Alice. Thank you!"

I hung up the phone and returned to the front desk to inform the team of our plan. Then I did what I dreaded. I walked up the three flights of stairs to Karl's office and broke the news to him.

Showing obvious disappointment, he asked, "Have you talked to the conference manager yet?"

"That's next."

He thanked me for letting him know and released me to return to recovery mode.

Next, I informed Megan, the hotel's conference manager. She, in turn, passed the update to the group contact.

No one was happy.

Alice, our housekeeping manager, worked a miracle. The beds were delivered in record time. They were cleaned, made, and placed in each guestroom before the group's dinner banquet at 7:00 p.m. Although we accommodated the guests in two beds, it was not the upscale, pampered experience they expected.

Despite our best—and heroic—efforts, the situation worsened.

Before and after the banquet, the front desk listened to many complaints from ladies who were not pleased with their sleeping arrangements.

"We reserved a room with two queen beds. *This* is not what we reserved."

"Do you actually expect me to sleep in this rusted old rollaway bed?"

"This is not acceptable. I'm not sleeping in this bed. You need to come up here right now and look at this."

Each time someone complained, the team members and I apologized profusely. We kindly let our guests know there were no other options.

By the second day, the complaints calmed. The ladies accepted the outcome and went on with their weekend. During their mass departure on Sunday, I was thankful that few complained about the arrangements as they checked out.

Monday morning, I received a call from Karl, our AGM. "Come see me."

Oh boy. I know what this is about.

I climbed the stairs, dreading each step.

Karl got quickly to the point, "Tell me what happened with the double-room inventory."

"I should have watched the inventory myself, especially since we were sold out this weekend. I informed the team, but they didn't realize our numbers were so tight. They changed numerous guests from single rooms to doubles, which left us short on doubles."

"I understand," Karl said. "You know, since it cost the hotel $3,000 in rental fees plus the $5,000 refund the group VIP demanded, plus the negative impact to our service, I have to document this for your file."

I felt a sinking feeling of disappointment. "I understand." I made no excuses. I couldn't.

He turned over a piece of paper and read the formal documentation. Then he handed it to me to sign. As I returned it to him, he smiled. "This will disappear from your file in six months. Don't worry about it."

I was grateful for his reassurance. "Thank you, Karl. This will not happen again."

And it didn't. I followed up regularly and implemented a new procedure to ensure we *all* had a process to manage the numbers daily.

Hospitality Hints

- ❖ Communicate pertinent information to your team.

- ❖ Follow up and inspect what you expect.

- ❖ Check in frequently when new or unusual procedures are introduced or required.

❖ As a leader, don't ever forget you are responsible for the actions and outcomes of your team.

❖ When you go to your manager with a problem, if possible, offer a solution as well.

❖ Manage your day, or your day will manage you.

17

Top Dogs

I dedicate this chapter to general managers and the differences in their management styles. Though the GMs I have worked with through the years were each as different as their favorite sport, they all had the same goal. Can you guess what that goal is?

The Looker

Christian Hansen was dreamy—a tall, athletic Norwegian who attended college in Oklahoma on a football scholarship. Interestingly, soccer was his favorite sport. Christian was a hands-on general manager. It wasn't unusual to see him in the breakfast kitchen with sleeves rolled up, giving the staff a hand—even washing dishes. He was a team player and a good guy.

He was also known to stop at every mirror he walked by to check his hair. Christian thought if you looked good and extended hospitality, everything from the kitchen duty down to the bottom line would fall into place. If he were a celebrity, he would be Tom Selleck from *Magnum, P.I.*, aka Monica's older boyfriend on the TV show *Friends*. Christian was a looker, that's for sure.

The Angry One

Randolf Thacker was mentored by a man who taught him to manage with an iron fist. As a result, he yelled often but was still respected and well-liked by his team. Our environment would have been much better for all of us—including Randolf and his gray hair—had he used less volume and a more conversational approach.

Randolf was a tall, slim man who resembled the actor Jimmy Stewart. Golf was his sport. He worked hard and ensured the hotel's success. In fact, under Randolf, our property won the coveted Hotel of the Year award. Randolf was also the GM during 9/11. He handled the event with strength and care.

He believed if you were aggressive, worked hard, and put in the time, your service scores and bottom line would reflect your efforts.

Randolf's nickname was Daddy Long Legs because of his tall stature.

Not Quite Ready

Chris Roberts was a nice young man but not ready for the position as general manager of our expansive conference center hotel. He came from a small boutique property in Hawaii, where he was very successful. I'm not sure of his favorite sport, but I do remember him going to town playing the air guitar at our holiday party—and he had not been drinking. So, maybe his favorite sport was not a sport at all, but music.

The demands of a conference center proved to be beyond Chris's ability at this time in his career. His previous experience didn't set him up to succeed. Unfortunately, the one who promoted Chris didn't recognize his need for growth. His new manager let him go after a single year.

Good Heart

Dan Moore was a kind gentleman. Football was his favorite sport. He always dressed as nicely as professional football players do when they travel. He kept us on our toes and held us accountable. When Dan approached someone, he always made a point to shake their hand. His smile and interest were genuine. Dan treated every team member as an essential part of our hotel family and saw the value each person brought. He was the kind of man who inspired loyalty from his team, me included. He was more interested in how we were doing personally than talking about work.

One memorable moment was the day Dan sought me out to apologize for telling what he later realized was an inappropriate joke earlier in the day. I appreciated his willingness to own his misstep, and it gave me a glimpse at the depth of his character.

Dan often said, "If you provide great service, everything else will fall into place." His catchphrase was "When it comes to the guest, the answer is *yes!*" Under Dan's leadership, the bottom line was always at or above budget.

If Dan were a celebrity, he would be a combination of the football player Howie Long and actor Rodney Dangerfield. An interesting combination.

Work Hard, Play Hard

Scott Hardy was a baseball fan. His permanent tan, the shade of strong tea, came from Florida, where he received his degree and where his heart will always be. He, too, was a kind gentleman. He managed in a fatherly way. He praised us when we did something right and counseled us when we needed it. Scott liked to spend time with his team. One of my favorite memories with Scott was when he took us managers bowling. Another was our managers' annual white elephant Christmas party. We had a lot of fun.

Scott is known for the phrase "Take the high road." In other words, no matter the circumstance, be professional and practice high standards. After our weekly staff meetings, Scott would often close the meeting by saying, "Keep your arms around 'em." It was his way of reminding us to be there for the guest. Follow-through and follow-up were important to Scott. During our time together, we experienced two recessions. Scott handled both with excellence. He led with solid strength and care for all involved.

Scott's nickname was Papa Bear.

Know that, as in any job, there will be a broad variety of personalities. As customer-facing employees, we must always be at our hospitable best. And at times, we have to manage behind the scenes with those for whom hospitality isn't a natural gift or ability.

Most general managers would agree: the service of those on the front line is what keeps the guests coming back. And it's the service that secures a solid bottom-line number.

So, what is the ultimate goal of a general manager? Is it service, or is it the bottom line?

You guessed it. It's both. They work in tandem.

Hospitality Hints

❖ Learn your manager's leadership style and adjust.

❖ Your attire and care for your appearance set the example for your team. Make it a priority.

❖ Hard work is essential. Without it, you'll never find success.

❖ Control your emotions. An iron fist is not necessary for effective management.

❖ Always be kind and respectful.

❖ Before promoting someone, be sure they are ready for the position.

❖ Always take the high road, follow up, and see things through.

18

I'm Sorry, the Answer
Is Still No

Policies aren't a guest favorite, but the nonnegotiable ones protect their safety and identity. An empowered front desk professional knows the art of saying no so creatively that the guest hears yes.

have yet to meet a guest who experiences joy when they hear the word *policy*. An exceptional front desk team will not only refrain from uttering the word, they will also practice empowerment and know when to modify a policy to fit a guest's needs.

There are, however, three policies for which empowerment does not apply. Learn more about these three, their catchphrases, and a few related scenarios on how to say yes when you're really saying no.

No ID, No Key

At the front desk, we use a consistent process to ensure a guestroom key is given only to the registered guest. Upon request of a key, the guest must present a government-issued ID (driver's license, ID card, passport, or military ID).

At check-in, be proactive and ask the guest if he would like to add the names of all adult occupants to his reservation. If he is off property all day, his family will be able to get a key without disturbing him.

The following are examples of defenses from guests who could not meet the security requirements to obtain a key:

The Name-Tagger

The hurried guest, on break from an in-house meeting, "But my name tag is my ID."

The Reciter

"I can tell you my address, phone number, and credit card number."

The Prankster

"I know I'm not registered to the bride and groom's room, but I just want to put something in the room before they arrive."

The Suspicious Spouse

"I know my name is not in your computer, but I'm his wife. We have the same last name."

Be especially careful with this one.

There is a way to say yes in most scenarios. Follow your hotel procedures on how to do so.

Secret Agent Sent to the Hotel

While in negotiations to host a women's Wimbledon pre-qualifier tennis tournament, the VIP for the potential celebrity group put the front desk team to the test. He asked for a key to his room and informed us he had no ID with him. For security purposes, we kindly agreed *if* he could tell us his room number. Only then would we have our security officer let him into his room to retrieve his ID and present it to be checked at the door.

Here's how we said yes. If the guest knows their room number, kindly inform them, "Our security officer is happy to open your room door to enable you to retrieve the ID and present it to the officer."

Confidential 411

Every piece of information on your reservation (name, address, phone number, stay dates) is confidential. On occasion, someone will try to obtain that information: a travel agent for commission purposes, an administrative assistant, a suspicious spouse. Whether the guest sounds innocent or not, they must positively identify themselves. At our property, a caller does this by giving the confirmation number or the last five digits of the credit card.

A scenario of when we have had to say no:

The Intimidator

At checkout, a female guest leaned over the desk and demanded that the front desk agent disclose the name and phone number of the occupants adjacent to her room. She said they kept her up arguing all night. "I am a lawyer, and I have the right to know their name and phone number!"

Divorce lawyer, no doubt.

The front desk agent kindly declined. Then, due to the guest's insistence, the manager got involved.

The manager's retort was subtle. "I have a degree in criminal justice, and you do not have the right to know. I'm sorry. We will not give you the information."

The guest stormed off.

There are times when you can't make it sound like yes. No means no.

No Pay, No Stay

Another strict policy is to ensure all guests pay for their stay in its entirety at check-in time. They must present the actual credit card. Below are examples of guests who tried to skirt around this policy. Thanks to good communication and training, the team didn't let them get too far.

The Criminal

Joan, a front desk supervisor, informed the young male guest his credit card authorization was declined. She also told him our policy required presenting the actual card. The guest held up his cell phone and scrolled through a list of over *twenty* credit card numbers from which to choose.

Joan, the front desk supervisor, responded, "I'm going to cancel your reservation. When you locate the actual card, we can reinstate the reservation. Have a nice day."

The guest and his female accomplice retreated. Problem solved.

Daddy's Boy

A local twenty-something guest, Robert Jones, presented his father's (also named Robert Jones) credit card at check-in. One month later, our accounting department received a call from Robert Jones Sr., who inquired about the $400 charge on his credit card bill.

Had the front desk agent compared the signature on the credit card to the ID, it would have been evident the card did not belong to Junior. The front desk agent then could have pointed out the mismatch and declined to accept it.

The best you can do is maintain a helpful attitude in most cases. Make no accusations and suggest it may be a simple mix-up. Offer whatever alternatives may be available.

One of several possible exceptions is to allow a known VIP to pay the next day upon receipt of a replacement of a lost credit card.

In the hotel industry, most policies are guidelines. They are what we call "gray." The three topics in this chapter are indeed policies. They are black-and-white, not gray.

In reality, the front desk agent wears many hats. Security and finance are two of the most important responsibilities. It's the department leader's responsibility to teach empowerment and the art of saying no in such a way that the guest hears yes.

I am sure you would agree: every guest should expect and pay for an experience that is both safe and enjoyable.

Hospitality Hints

❖ You are responsible for your guests' safety.

❖ You are responsible for verified payment collection.

❖ Positively identify each guest before you disclose information.

❖ If you must say no, let the guest know what you *can* do first.

❖ Never let a guest intimidate you. Request assistance if needed.

19

Hidden Perils of Progress

Change in an organization can create many positive aspects. It can encourage innovation, develop skills, and generate better business opportunities, leading to maintaining a competitive edge. But that isn't always the outcome. What happens when a change harms your daily operation?

Radia

Our new assistant GM, Karl, appreciated quality and advanced technology. Soon after joining the team, he researched ways to improve our communication system. At the time, our PBX operator and department managers used two-way radios, aka walkie-talkies. The radios worked well. With the press of a button, we were in instant contact with any of our coworkers. If we asked one team member to complete a task and it was closer to another, the other would jump in and say, "I've got it."

The radios were a win for the team and for servicing the guests promptly.

Upon completing his research, Karl signed a contract with Radia, a communications company that mainly catered to hospitals. Their candy-bar-sized device replaced our two-way radios.

Soon after training and implementation, I learned Radia was *not* as positive a change as expected. Radia didn't offer the same ease of use as our two-way radios. Instead, Radia became a middleman that required us to talk to her before anyone else. Here is an example:

Me: "Call Pat Allen"
Radia: "You would like to call Pat Allen, right?"
Me: "Yes."
Radia: "Calling Pat Allen."
Pause.
Pat finally answers. We talk. Call is over.

More often than not, communication was difficult and added an unnecessary delay in reaching the intended party. At times, Radia even seemed argumentative. If I asked her to call someone with a not-so-easy-to-pronounce name, I could forget it. At that point, it was easier to walk down the hall and talk to Raymond Jabbernathy in person.

Regardless of Radia's adverse effect on our communication and service, Karl insisted we continue its use. To some, it appeared that his preference to prove himself right and the monetary investment already made prevented him from discontinuing the new service. Radia was here to stay.

After some research of my own, I came upon an online review of Radia that read, "I want to take this device out to the parking lot and run over it ten times with my car!"

We knew their pain.

Three years into our relationship with Radia, push-to-talk cell phones debuted. They were similar to two-way radios.

The new technology piqued Karl's interest. So, we broke up with Radia, citing irreconcilable differences, and made the change to cell phones. We all were relieved.

Check-in Kiosk

Of all the hotel chains I could work for, I would still choose my twenty-five-year favorite all over again. Of course, no company is perfect, but I've seen enough to know ours is as close as it gets. Technology integration is one of our corporation's strong qualities.

Years ago, the corporate office introduced the check-in kiosk. It's an ATM look-alike that guests used to check in. They could type in their information on the touchscreen, and *voila*, the key dropped into a dispensing tray. It was a simple alternative to the front desk—even though, at first look, it could appear intimidating.

The purchase of at least one kiosk was mandatory for all properties.

We did our best to persuade guests to use the metal front desk agent but soon learned the machine lacked one crucial attribute: the human touch.

Because of guest resistance to using the kiosks, our corporate office mandated hotels to increase use to 30 percent within ninety days of implementation. We did our best to raise our numbers. I even called a neighboring hotel to ask how they persuaded guests to use the faux front desk agent.

"The guests still come to us at the front desk," my cohort reported. "We just walk over and check them in at the kiosk ourselves."

Human preference triumphed over innovation. The expensive initiative fizzled out after one year.

Help Desk Offshore

Our new CEO's primary task was to turn the company around financially. One of his initiatives was to move our Tennessee-based technical support offshore—to another country.

The language and cultural barriers, combined with the new offshore team's need to read from a manual *while on the phone with us*, made it impossible to receive the prompt help we needed. Our conversations with a technician became a perpetual frustration.

When the computer system crashed in the middle of a long line of guests, the communication barriers worked against us.

I'm not one to let my frustration show, but I've ended a call with support more than once to look up and find my team staring at me wide-eyed and silent from hearing my impatient replies.

During one conversation, I insisted, "I will not answer your questions again. You've asked me the same question four times, and we've been on the phone for only ten minutes."

After several years of frustration and complaints from the staff, general managers company-wide took our grievances to their annual convention.

The staff in the corporate office used the feedback they received to implement changes for the offshore support team. Unfortunately, their modifications were like running fresh water through a bucket with a hole in it—not effective.

Over the years, our corporate office has implemented many great initiatives. Due to the negative impact on service and the delay in resolving issues, the offshore experiment was *not* one of them.

In an effort to continue to manage costs, the system is still in place. There are still challenges with it, but the staff has learned to utilize it as well as possible.

Industries everywhere that balance customers' needs—both internal and external—and manage the bottom line are often in conflict. Having to live with a less-than-perfect system may someday land where you are as well. Learning how to patiently and professionally handle this type of situation now will make you one step ahead.

Hospitality Hints

❖ Avoid change for change's sake. Think it through and include all pertinent team members in the planning process, including hourly employees who work on the front lines.

❖ As a whole, guests will always want human interaction. The front desk agent is here to stay.

❖ Even if you don't like or agree with a new initiative, stay positive, and help your team adjust. A negative attitude produces negative results. A positive attitude produces positive results.

20

The One with All the Snakes

Every hotel has a unique challenge. It's up to each management team to pursue a resolution that enhances guest comfort and builds their trust.

Ahotel up the street from ours has a plumbing issue so severe they have to leave a hot water faucet continually running in the basement from 6:00 a.m. to 11:00 p.m. Otherwise, the hot water won't flow to the guestrooms. Can you imagine the water bill?

You might ask, "What was your hotel's unique issue?" I will tell you, but first, I must say the stories I share with you are from my first few years at the property. This unique challenge has long since been resolved.

Parking lots surround most hotels in our area. Though well-land-scaped, they are still parking lots. We're fortunate to have a property on scenic wooded acreage alongside a small, quiet lake. With the beautiful lake and nature comes wildlife. We have a range from grace-ful deer to timid armadillos to slithery snakes. Yes, you heard right: *snakes*. And that, my dear reader, was our unique challenge.

I assure you that no guest has ever been seriously injured by a snake on our property. But we did have a challenge keeping those little creatures outside.

If you're like me, you get the creeps when someone even mentions the word *snake*. For that reason, I will spare you—and me—from excessive detail as I share a few memorable run-ins.

Just Kidding. No, Really!

"Very funny, Donnie." Sarah, the front desk agent, glared at the bellman.

"What?" He turned his head to look at her.

With her hand on her hip, she smirked. "The fake snake you put in the gift shop."

Donnie's brows knit together as he tilted his head. "What are you talking about?" He went to investigate.

A few guests shopped on the far side of the store as Donnie and Sarah entered the gift shop. Donnie looked down at the snake curled up on the floor just inside the door. He grabbed a basket off the shelf faster than lightning and slammed it down over the curled-up creature.

Out of breath, he mouthed. "It's real!"

Sarah paled and stifled a shriek.

Donnie stayed with the contained reptile while Sarah quickly reported a *Code D* (dangerous creature) to our engineer, aka snake wrangler. His quick thinking made it much easier for engineering to remove the intruder. And that he did—swiftly. Once all was clear, Donnie and Sarah went back to work. The guests were none the wiser.

Nowhere to Run, Nowhere to Hide

Two ladies, strangers to one another, stepped inside an elevator. The doors shut.

Suddenly, the casually dressed lady politely asked the professionally dressed lady, "Can you step over here?"

The other woman maintained protocol for elevator silence and stayed still as a statue.

In a calm, careful tone, the casually dressed lady spoke again, "Ma'am, can you just step over to this side of the elevator, please?"

The woman looked at her puzzled but remained still.

One more try.

"Ma'am, there's a snake by your foot!"

The business-like lady moved so fast that she nearly jumped into the woman's arms. The commotion in the elevator scared the snake so badly that it slithered up the wall behind a panel. Seconds later, the door opened, and both ladies burst out.

After the incident, the ladies, now having bonded, went as a team to report the companion elevator rider to the front desk. The front desk agent promptly called the engineering department, not masking her surprise and concern. When engineering arrived at the scene, he cautiously peeked around in the elevator. However, he never did find the hidden reptile. Since the incident, I am sure to peek into an elevator before I step inside.

Blinky

Rather than handling the situation herself, a cautious housekeeper reported what she thought was a fake snake in a planter at the indoor pool. Joey, our guest service manager, and I hurried downstairs and took the opportunity to perk up our day and assist engineering.

The four of us gathered three feet away from the planter and leaned forward to peer in. Engineering stepped back and removed a pool pole from the wall. He used it to pick up the snake carefully.

Keeping our distance, we encircled the motionless, dangling creature.

"It doesn't *look* real." The housekeeper squinted as she looked on.

"It's hard to tell." The engineer kept the pole steady.

Joey pointed at the snake and blurted, "No, it's real! I just saw it blink."

I looked closer and squinted. *Can a snake blink?*

Engineering slowly laid the snake on the tiled floor. After further inspection and discussion, we agreed that snakes *could* blink, but only if they were real. Fortunately, this one was not.

Who put the snake in the planter? We will never know.

Hospitality Hints

❖ Train and coach your team to be prepared to respond to guests appropriately—no matter the issue. Your team may not be as experienced as you are, and they need your guidance.

❖ When a guest reports a persistent issue (for example, a repetitive bug or plumbing issue), just short of a gasp, react as if it has never happened before, apologize, then take action.

❖ No matter what issues your property may face, seek a resolution until you find one.

❖ You've heard the old saying, "The leak doesn't get fixed until it drips on the boss's desk."

❖ Don't be that kind of boss.

21

Key Card Conundrum

It started as a typical Friday. I arrived at 2:00 p.m., checked the details of the day, and received a briefing from the previous manager. All indicators suggested a quiet, uneventful night, or so I thought.

Shortly after I settled into my office, James, our front desk agent, stuck his head through the door. "Kim, we can't make keys." He smirked, expressing his disappointment in this all-too-frequent event.

I looked up from my desk. "How long has the interface been down?"

"Five minutes."

"Okay. I'll call tech support. For now, make keys through the key program."

I went through the usual steps with our help desk. Nothing they tried worked. Then, I caught Jeff, our IT manager.

"Before you go home for the day, Jeff, can you check the server? Support was unable to help."

Puzzled, Jeff reported, "Everything seems to be working properly."

Hmmm. That's what support said. Not what I wanted to hear.

I reassured Jeff. "We're not busy tonight. Go ahead and call it a day. I'll call you if it's not working by morning."

"Okay. I hate to say it, but I'm going out of town tonight and won't be back until Sunday."

"It's okay. I'll call tech support again if needed."

Though it slowed down the check-in process, making keys through the key system wasn't difficult. I knew we would manage through the night just fine.

It happens on occasion. Surely the interface will reset and work again after the night audit. I propped up my confidence and headed home.

But upon my arrival the next day, the key interface was still down.

I placed a second call to support. Their efforts were again unsuccessful. I returned to the front desk just in time to face a new dilemma: one guest after the next returned to say their key didn't work. Since master keys *did* work, bellmen and security quickly jumped in to escort guests to their rooms.

Amid the chaos, I asked Nick, our security officer, to call his manager at home. "Please ask Mark to come in to check his side of the system. It's the only thing we haven't ruled out."

I sensed Nick's aggravation. "I already called. He isn't coming. He commanded us to continue to walk guests to their rooms."

Oh, he didn't want his three-day weekend interrupted. I nodded. "I understand. I'll see what I can do. On another note, our fail-safe keys binder is in the safe. It holds two master keys for every guestroom. Be sure to save them as a last resort."

"Oh, we tested the fail-safe keys, and they don't work."

Not what I wanted to hear. *We will address that issue later.*

I enlisted Angela, our HR director, to help convince Mark we needed him on property. Angela made the call, but to my dismay, she reported Mark would not be in until Monday due to a conflict.

By the end of the day, the bellmen and security crew were run ragged, and the front desk team was exhausted. I departed feeling uneasy but knowing the overnight staff would manage the situation until I returned the next morning. And best of all, our IT manager would be back in town. Surely, he could resolve the issue.

Sunday

Jeff arrived mid-morning and went straight to work in our closet-sized server room. After two hours of troubleshooting, he reluctantly delivered the bad news, "There's nothing more I can do. We need Mark on property. The problem has to be his side of the system."

Somehow, I knew that's what he would say.

As the key challenges continued at the front desk, James, the front desk agent who initially reported the issue, was so perplexed that he sat down, stared at the floor, shook his head, and said to himself over and over, "How can this be happening?"

Keeping my mutual feelings hidden, I assured him that we would get through this.

Monday

Mid-morning, while behind the front desk and feeling thankful for a short reprieve before the afternoon rush, I noticed Mark, our missing-in-action security chief, stroll across the lobby toward me.

Frustration contained, I greeted him politely. "Hi, Mark. Thank you for coming in."

Short and to the point, he said, "Make me a key to an unoccupied room." Key in hand, he turned and walked toward the guestroom tower.

Five minutes later, Mark startled me as he tossed the key on the desk next to my hand. "It doesn't work!"

The nerve. No kidding. It didn't work the other three hundred times this weekend either.

Containing my frustration, I nodded. "I know."

"I'll go check a few locks." He grumbled, then turned toward his office.

"Thanks, Mark." Still calm.

He returned thirty minutes later. "You're gonna have to call Jeff back. I don't know what's going on." And just like that, he was gone.

All resources exhausted, I called our key system support one more time and insisted they fly someone out to resolve this significant guest-service interruption. To my surprise, they complied, no question.

There's hope for tomorrow!

Tuesday

The managers who had been off during this holiday weekend nightmare returned to experience firsthand what we endured all weekend long. To their credit, they jumped in to help the bellmen and security crew escort guests to their rooms.

Upon the evening arrival of the support team, relief set in. It was the first deep breath I'd taken in days. They immediately went to work, logging late hours into the night, then back at it again early the next morning.

Wednesday

At 7:00 a.m., behind the front desk, Doug, the support rep, assured me all would be fixed by mid-morning. Minutes later, Mark approached Doug.

I stepped over and joked, "Hey, Mark. What's up? Are you slowing down my help?"

His usual dry response, "No, I just had a question."

Seconds later, Mark asked. "Can I talk to you for a minute?" He motioned for me to step out into the lobby, then walked around the corner. I followed.

Without warning, he pointed his finger an inch from my face, his brow cinched and lips pursed. "Don't you *ever* belittle me like that again."

I stepped back. "What?" *Where did this come from?*

He repeated, "Don't you ever belittle me again."

What are you talking about? Oh, it's my "distracting the help" remark.

Stunned, I explained, "Mark, I was joking."

"No, you weren't." He leaned in and scowled, "There's always truth in jokes."

My tone suggested he back off. "Mark, I was joking. Lighten up."

"There are only two people I answer to in this hotel: Mr. Beck and Mr. Hardy"—the AGM and GM.

Okay, you're going to state facts. Here are some facts.

"Mark, you are not my boss. And you will not talk to me the way you talk to your team."

119

Rattled a bit, I turned toward the front desk and walked away. I don't know what Mark did or where he went. I did not look back.

As promised, the system was up and running mid-day. The issue was at last resolved.

The support rep determined a server glitch on Friday had started the issue. And it was made worse by a support error on Saturday.

Though many were involved, none were more relieved than the front desk team. The daily operation quickly returned to normal. Well, mostly normal.

Mark and I intentionally avoided each other, only interacting during necessary collaborations. It was months before the tension eased.

Hospitality Hints

❖ Be proficient in the workings of your computer servers. Small mistakes can cause big issues.

❖ Handle all matters with a service-first attitude and strategy. It will minimize guest complaints.

❖ All managers are on the same team. Help each other resolve issues.

❖ Be careful about joking during stressful times. Relationships are important.

❖ Never make a person the brunt of a joke. Be considerate of others' feelings.

22

Could I Not Have This Dance

We're all asked to participate in things that take us out of our comfort zone from time to time. Doing so is an integral part of our growth. I recall one time when I not only stepped out of my comfort zone but also stepped out of my comfort galaxy.

Our property was host to one of Texas's most prestigious wine industry events: the Texas Wine Tribute Gala and Auction, a city-sponsored, black-tie event held in the Grand Ballroom.

The magnitude of the event required the assistance of every department manager. What position did we hold? Dancing sommeliers.

Because of the unusual nature of the request, the job offer letter given to every new manager included a clause detailing their mandatory participation in the gala. Most, including me, have tried to talk, or *plead*, their way out of it. None have succeeded.

The gala began with the arrival of the who's who of our city. There was a brief reception in our lobby where we served each guest their first glass of wine. They then made their way up the grand staircase to the extravagantly decorated ballroom located on the mezzanine level. My colleagues and I waited anxiously in the adjoining hallway behind closed doors.

Once the guests were seated at the tables adorned in decadence, the emcee, usually a local television celebrity, offered a warm welcome and ten minutes of announcements for the evening's events. During this time, the managers, aka dancing sommeliers, would sneak out, move into the main hallway and line up in four rows at the still-closed Grand Ballroom entrance doors. The first person in each row listened for our cue from the emcee, their ear pressed against the door as the other managers shushed each other.

"And now, ladies and gentlemen, the dancing sommeliers!"

The music started, the four sets of double doors swung open, and we danced our way into the ballroom—backs straight, chins up, napkin on each tuxedoed arm, a chilled bottle of wine in hand.

Midway through the song and dance, we paused at our assigned tables and offered the first pour. Our nervous hands trembled—or at least mine did—as we carefully moved from one guest's wine glass to the next.

At last, we poured the eighth glass. We resumed the dance, making our way back together and exiting just as festively as we entered. Applause ushered us out as we hustled to prepare for the next round. The dance was, at last, complete.

Thanks to her previous dance training, Julie, the GM's admin, served as our choreographer. During our first dance rehearsal one year, Julie divided us into four rows as we stood at the back of the ballroom. Mark, our security manager and someone I tried to avoid because of our previous conflict, ended up right in front of me. *At least he's in front. It would be even more awkward if he were behind me.*

Julie continued her instruction. "Now, everyone, walk in time to the music toward the front of the room. When you reach the front, stop and gather in a circle."

We half-hearted managers slowly made our way to the front. I stood in what passed for a circle and noticed Mark to my left.

"Very good! Now, in this part, we want to simulate a clock," Julie continued. "You will do this by putting your arms around each other to close the circle and . . ."

Wait! Put our arms around each other?

"… dance in one full rotation clockwise."

We've never had to put our arms around each other. And you wait until I'm next to Mark?

She continued as my mind raced. I tried to figure a way out. I looked in Mark's direction. He also had that searching-for-an-out look.

I knew there was nothing I could do. My angst quickly turned to silent laughter. I realized that only the God of the universe could have arranged this. *It was meant to be.*

Okay, Mark. I'm ready for you, buddy.

I turned my head, gave him a sideways glance, and raised my arms. He raised his. May the force be with us. And we both stepped—together—into a brand-new galaxy.

Hospitality Hints

❖ As one of my favorite humorists, Jeanne Robertson, says, "Find the humor in everything."[2] HR will appreciate it.

❖ Sometimes challenges at work look intimidating. Accept them as opportunities to grow. You are stronger than you know.

❖ At work, as in life, there may be people who get under our skin. Learn to manage your personal feelings and maintain a cordial and collaborative approach. Uphold your professionalism at all times.

❖ Keep those dancing shoes close at hand. You never know when you might need them.

23

The Power of a
Telephone Operator

Our PBX operator received a call that could close the gap between making our annual budget or failing to do so. But did she realize the power she had to make or break the deal?

It's no secret that Texans don't do snow. When the first flake hits the ground, businesses close, people ransack grocery stores, and schools shut down—at which point children break out into dance—the sprinkler dance. Our big trucks and big confidence turn into the big strong elephant that shrinks at the sight of a mouse. This Christmas weekend was no exception. The weatherman predicted the worst: three inches of accumulation overnight, enough to build a cowboy snowman.

That was all the general manager needed to hear. So, we shifted into emergency weather mode and did what managers do best. We had a meeting.

Who's going to lay rock salt? Who will place caution signs? Who will be here in the morning? Will the PM team be able to drive home?

All these questions were asked and answered before the meeting in the GM's office broke up. We would salt our sidewalks and decorate our floors with caution signs. Guests would have hot coffee in the morning and a front desk agent to serve them at the front desk. We were ready for the imminent blizzard.

One of my duties was to manage a block of rooms for team members, including myself, to stay the night and avoid driving on slick roads. After our game plan was in place, I made a quick drive home for an overnight bag. Upon returning to the hotel, I went to my room, finished my last-minute Christmas shopping online, and silently thanked the retailers for priority shipping. Finally, I snuggled in tight for a good night's sleep to face the day ahead.

◆ ◆ ◆

Rachel, the front desk agent, and I were at the front desk early the next morning. We both stood there and gazed out the lobby windows to a winter wonderland. The blanket of snow was breathtaking. And as promised, the overnight storm hit hard. We could indeed build our cowboy snowman.

"Thanks for the room, Kim. I don't think I could have made it driving in. Look at it out there."

"I know. Same here. But isn't it beautiful?"

At the start of the day, Rachel and I assisted departing guests with checking their flights and handled calls from guests needing to cancel their reservations.

Overall, the hotel's year was successful, but we were forecast to end under budget. The cancellations only added to the deficit.

Mid-morning, Carol, our PBX operator, called me at the front desk. "Kim, a lady is on the phone and wants to speak to a sales manager. It's regarding rooms this weekend. I didn't tell her the sales office is closed. Are you available?"

"Yes, of course. Give me one minute, then transfer the call to my desk."

Happy to be off my feet, I picked up the phone and greeted the caller.

"Hi, Kim, my name is Susan. I'm with FedEx and need to talk to you about a block of rooms for this weekend."

"Hi, Susan, I am happy to help you." Knowing our occupancy was low, I continued. "I am sure we can accommodate your request."

"I hope you can. We need at least three hundred rooms, starting tomorrow."

Three hundred rooms? I scrambled for a pen.

She explained. "Due to the snowstorm and the increase in online Christmas shopping, my company plans to fly district managers from all over the country to DFW. They will assist our delivery team to ensure everyone's packages arrive before Christmas."

I requested Susan's contact information. "Susan, I am certain we can secure a contract today. I will call Joyce, our director of sales, right away."

After a few more minutes of discussion, I hung up with Susan and called Joyce. She, too, was floored at the large piece of last-minute business that had just landed in our lap. The ball was now in her hands to run it for a sales touchdown.

After wrapping things up with Joyce, I walked over to Carol, our operator. "Good job, Carol! That call was for a large block of rooms starting tomorrow. She requested seventy-five percent of our room inventory. Thank you for connecting the call to me and not the sales voicemail."

Minutes later, Joyce called me back, "Kim, I'm writing the contract as we speak. Call all the department heads and tell them we need all hands on deck tomorrow for three hundred arrivals. The group will be here for five nights."

I made the calls. We adjusted our schedules and made it happen. This piece of business closed the gap between our revenue goal and the forecasted discrepancy. We ended the year in the green.

Touchdown!

I was excited to have been a part of securing this much-needed piece of business. I got to experience first-hand the rush of exhilaration a sales manager feels when a client signs a contract.

After all was said and done, Carol received a special recognition award from our general manager. He commended her for a job well done and for understanding the importance and urgency of every phone call, specifically the urgent call for our sales department during the snowstorm.

I have a new respect for FedEx. Instead of shrugging off the delay of their customers' packages, they did what they had to do and made Christmas possible for us last-minute online shoppers. I was also glad the FedEx managers made it home in time for Christmas with their families.

It was an exciting and memorable time. And like the school children at the news of a snow day, we too did the sprinkler dance.

Hospitality Hints

❖ Every call received at PBX is important. Unless a caller asks for someone by name, qualify the call by asking a question or two to ensure you transfer it to the right person.

❖ Train the operators on what to do if a sales manager is unavailable.

❖ Check in with PBX throughout the day and help when they are busy.

❖ Just as FedEx recognized the importance of their customers' satisfaction, recognize a job well done by your team.

❖ Staff is often a hotel's number one expense and is always a hotel's number one asset. Don't skimp here.

24

Talk to the Hand

It's ingrained in hoteliers to be kind and consistently offer excellent service to guests, which is vital to repeat business and guest loyalty. Never in my wildest dreams would I have thought I'd seemingly go against the grain and tell a guest, "Talk to the hand!"

I t was check-in day for a group of four hundred beauticians. The lobby was bursting at the seams with guests and their luggage. Not the best time for a computer outage, which created lines that extended from the check-in desk to the hotel entrance.

The front desk team worked feverishly in manual check-in mode. The assistant manager, Tonya, helped each front desk agent find vacant rooms from the paper room list in her hand. Her long black hair flew behind her with each change in direction. I'm sure she regretted her decision to wear three-inch heels on this day.

I was on the phone with our computer help desk in the office behind the guest check-in area. It was nearing my *second* hour on the phone when Heidi, the general manager's administrative assistant, came from the front desk through the office door. Tonya was hot on her heels. I could tell by the serious looks on their faces and quick steps that they were on a mission. It was obvious they had something to say. Sure enough, Heidi bent down close to my face and said in whispered anger, "Kim, that troublemaker is back."

I knew exactly who she was talking about. Mr. Weaver, the man who harassed Tonya because room service sent up the wrong brand of champagne during his recent visit. We thought the case was closed when he checked out the day before. We did not charge him for his order and had sent up our best bottle on the house. What more could a guest want, right? It was very unusual for someone to return after checkout to continue a complaint.

Determined not to lose my connection with the help desk, I handed Heidi the phone, looked her in the eye, and said sternly, "You stay on this phone and *do not* let them hang up. I'll be right back."

I got up from the chair and turned to Tonya, "Show me where he is."

We marched toward the lobby. Tonya pointed to the casually dressed middle-aged man who stood just beyond the front desk. She stayed behind as I made my way through the crowded reception area. My hands remained at my side as I approached the complainer. I looked him in the eye. "Mr. Weaver, my name is Kim Annington. I'm the front office manager. How may I help you?"

He pointed to Tonya. "No. I want to talk to her!"

I had no time or approval for this attempt at continued harassment.

I shot my hand up in protest, palm facing him. "The only person you will talk to at this point is security."

With my hand still in place, I looked to my left at David, the security officer, who had already begun to make his way over. I turned back to the guest. To my surprise, he had retreated and was halfway to the front door.

Admittedly, I was disappointed that security didn't have a chance to make it unmistakably clear to Mr. Weaver that we did not tolerate bullies. The guest apparently figured that out on his own.

I returned to the phone. Heidi had followed my instructions to the letter and hadn't let the help desk disconnect the call. Security returned to oversee the crowd, and Tonya went back to help the front desk agents.

It didn't dawn on me until later that evening what I had actually done. After the computers were fixed, several of us gathered behind the front desk to catch our breath from the historic computer outage. Suddenly Tonya announced, "Kim told a guest to talk to the hand."

The room filled with laughter. It was rather out of character for me and never okay in the service industry. But this time was an exception. Remember the gray areas mentioned in the chapter, "I'm Sorry the Answer is Still No"? Well, that certainly applied here. Never tell a guest to talk to the hand—unless he is harassing your employee.

With my actions that day, I gained superhero status with my team. Never had I said or done anything like it, and I never would again. They knew it, and so did I. We all knew it was a once-in-a-career-time moment.

Hospitality Hints

* ❖ Never allow a guest to bully a team member. It's always the right thing to intercede and protect your staff. Standing up for your team has an added benefit: it will increase the level of respect they already have for you. They will feel supported and valued. Valuing and supporting your team increases loyalty and motivation.

* ❖ Coach your team on how to handle different types of guest interactions. Help them know at what point they politely excuse themselves to get your help.

* ❖ Have a contingency plan in place for computer outages. Do your best to make the interruption unnoticeable to guests.

25

A Cup of Humor

Upon arrival at the hotel, I'm often met with a humorous or unbelievable story from someone on the previous shift. This day would be no exception.

As Amy stepped through the front desk door, Kelly, another front desk agent, asked, "How was your lunch?"

"It was all right." Amy exaggerated her southern drawl. "The cafeteria served corn dogs and french fries. I had a salad." She laughed.

The conversation was interrupted by the sound of luggage wheels as they thumped across the faux brick floor.

"Looks like we have more early check-ins," Kelly groaned.

Amy looked up at the three cowboys walking toward her, luggage in hand. "Oh my." She stayed at her workstation as Kelly stepped three feet over to hers, never taking her eyes off the guests.

The three men rounded the corner of the water feature in the center of the lobby.

"I've got the tall one," Amy said out of the side of her mouth.

The men dropped their luggage on and around the nearby chairs. They straightened, then turned toward the front desk.

Amy smiled and cheerfully greeted them as they approached. "Hi. How are y'all today?"

"We're doing great." The tall one spoke up as he walked toward the desk. As he approached Kelly, Amy's countenance dropped but recovered quickly as she turned to welcome one of the other two. "This is a nice place." The guest continued. He nodded as he looked around.

"Why, thank you. My name is Kelly. This is Amy."

"My name is Troy Allen." He motioned to his friends. "This is Billy Powell and Leroy Cupp. We call him Bubba."

"Welcome, gentlemen," Kelly typed Mr. Allen's name in the computer.

Amy assisted Bubba while Billy waited his turn.

"So, what brings y'all to the area?" Amy asked.

Bubba spoke up. "We're on a hunting trip."

"Oh. Is that right?" Amy looked behind them and noticed what appeared to be rifle cases among their luggage. "I noticed your gun cases. Do you mind if I have our security officer hold them for you? He will lock them in a secure storage room until you check out."

"Nope, we don't mind at all." Mr. Allen said. "We plan to leave early in the morning."

"That's all right. Our officers are here twenty-four hours a day." Amy picked up the phone and made a quick call. After she set the phone down, she looked up. "Sorry about the wait. I'll get you checked in now."

Kelly handed Mr. Allen his room key. He stood by as the others checked in.

Amy typed, squinting at the monitor. "May I ask how you spell your last name? I am having difficulty finding it on the computer."

"Oh, sure. It's c-u-p-p."

Amy repeated each letter as she typed. "C-u-p-p."

Bubba leaned in, his belly squishing against the counter. "Yeah. It's c-u-p-p." He paused. "But I didn't really see you pee-pee." He cackled and waited for a response.

Amy's shoulders dropped. She and Kelly giggled and shook their heads as they looked at each other.

"Put *him* in the basement." Mr. Allen spoke up.

Billy joined in, "Yeah, put him as far away from us as possible."

Amy noticed Kyle, our security officer, had arrived to store their rifles. He stood at attention behind the guests with a grin on his face. He, too, was amused.

"Thank you, Mr. Cupp. I found it. But I think I should start calling you Bubba." Amy giggled. "So, where are ya'll going hunting?"

"We're on our way to East Texas. This is the halfway point."

"Well, we're glad ya'll stopped in for a visit. Here's your room key. Your tower is to your right. Be sure to let us know if you need anything."

Amy motioned to the security officer. "Kyle is here to store your things."

Kelly handed Billy his room key. The three men turned toward their luggage.

"Gentlemen, I'm here to assist you with your gun cases. I'm happy to store them until you check out. You may pick them up any time."

After giving Kyle their firearms, he instructed, "Here are your claim tickets. Just let the front desk know when you're ready to retrieve your items."

Kyle loaded the heavy cases onto the cart and turned toward the elevator. The guests threw their bags over their shoulders. As they turned toward their room tower, Amy joked, "Oh, Kyle, don't forget to escort Bubba to the basement."

Hospitality Hints

❖ Smile, laugh, and have fun with guests. Know where to draw the line. If it's crossed—in this case, it was not—a good response is silence or breaking eye contact and continuing your work.

❖ Always stay professional.

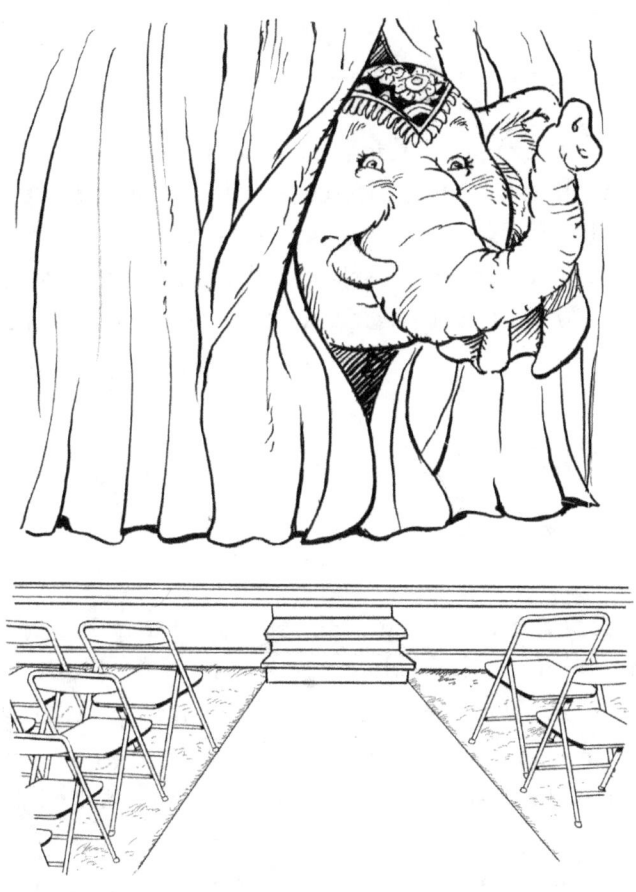

26

An Elephant Walks
into a Wedding

It isn't standard practice for us to add services to a group's itinerary unless it's agreed upon prior to their event. A water feature was not in this wedding party's plans. How would our team recover from an unwanted hydration experience?

It was the third and most meaningful day of the vibrant, intricately planned Hindu wedding. The stage was set on our lush green back lawn overlooking the lake. Bold-colored linen draped down the four corners of the platform's ceiling. The bride and groom's regal gold chairs were positioned near the front. Two hundred white padded chairs were perfectly set in front of the platform for the guests. The red carpet would soon be rolled out. Above it all was clear blue Texas sky. It was a perfect day.

The previous two days consisted of mini ceremonies between the bride and groom's families that beautifully ushered in the main ceremony.

Christie, the catering manager, ran around the property getting pulled from every side. This day—full of culture-rich festivities, celebration, and tradition—had to be perfect.

The procession known as the *baraat* would begin in the hotel lobby, where the groomsmen dressed in traditional brilliant-colored tunics gather around the groom, singing and dancing to celebrate the upcoming ceremony. They would make their way out the front door toward—get ready—a massive, beautiful elephant adorned with jewels to match the groom's attire. The gentle giant would carry him to meet his bride.

Many guests paused to observe the festivities. It isn't every day you see an elephant at a hotel, especially in Texas.

Curious, I researched elephant rental. It's recommended to reserve your elephant first, a year in advance, *then* pick your venue. Elephants for hire are not easy to come by.

Before the baraat started, I walked to the back of the hotel to a large window that overlooked the stage. As I rounded the corner of the hall, I saw several guests with their noses to the glass, oohing and aahing. I slipped in with them to take a peek.

The beautiful display of colors was a banquet for the eyes. Several members of the bride and groom's families stood talking in clusters across the lawn. I looked down to see a small crowd enjoying a refreshing drink near the door where the bride would make her first appearance.

Of all weddings our property has hosted, this was the most spectacular.

As I took in the beauty, I noticed Susan and Armondo, our event managers, adding a few additional chairs to the setup.

Knowing the groom's celebration dance would begin soon in the lobby, I turned to go back to the front desk. I was two steps away when I heard the onlookers at the window gasp. I whipped back around to see. *Did someone fall? Is everyone ok?* I poked my head between the people in front of me.

Oh no! The sprinkler system had turned on! Right in the middle of the chairs!

I turned around and bolted downstairs. I smiled and kept my composure as I passed guests in the hall. When I got to the exit door downstairs, Susan stood inside, her hair and face dripping wet. Out of breath, she held the radio to her mouth, "Engineering, come in! Engineering, come in!"

"Go ahead."

"Turn the sprinklers off! TURN THE SPRINKLERS OFF!"

Susan ran to housekeeping down the hall and grabbed a cart full of towels. She and the housekeeping attendant rushed back with the cart. We filled our hands, straightened our backs, composed ourselves as much as possible, then beelined it to the wet chairs. We spread out and wiped one chair at a time until all two hundred were dry. Embarrassed, I looked up only once at the family who stood nearby. Somehow it didn't seem to faze them. They were fully engaged in their conversations.

When she was satisfied with our cleanup efforts, Susan caught my attention and that of the others from a few rows up. She tilted her head and mouthed, "Let's go."

As we walked away from the chairs toward the building, the ushers began seating the guests. I cringed as I watched the first ladies sit down in their beautiful sari gowns.

Please don't be wet.

To my relief, everyone stayed seated. No one jumped up in surprise at a damp seat.

Christie, the catering manager, caught us as we entered the door. "Thank you, guys. I'll see what happened to our communication with the grounds men later." She stayed downstairs for the bride's arrival.

Susan, Armondo, and the housekeeping attendant pushed the cart of wet towels back to housekeeping. They would dry *themselves* off while there. I caught my breath and walked toward the elevator. On my way up, I looked down at my new black leather pumps, which were now soaking wet.

Oh well, a small price to pay for saving the day.

I was happy to have made it to the lobby in time for the groom's baraat celebration. It was more merriment and activity than our lobby had ever seen in the morning hours. As the joyful group of men sang, danced, and cheered their way out the front door, I zipped back to the hotel's floor-to-ceiling rear window. The same crowd of guests was still there.

Only a few minutes later, we saw the groom enter on his majestic elephant. Adorned in elegant fabric and jewelry, the beautiful creature carried the groom toward the ceremony, every step slow and magnificent.

Once they reached the stopping point, the groom descended and walked down the red carpet to the stage to await his bride. Shortly thereafter, directly below the window where I stood, the bride in her crimson dress walked gracefully down the stairs toward the red carpet. On her proud father's arm, she approached her groom. The two ascended the stairs to the platform and took their seats. After many more hours of ceremony, the young couple were pronounced man and wife.

Hospitality Hints

❖ It's best for all department heads to attend staff meetings, especially for an event with unusual requirements that may be unfamiliar to staff. Communication is the key to success.

❖ When you communicate details, be sure you have the attention of the one receiving the information.

❖ Follow up and double-check essential requirements before the big event. Never assume.

❖ If something goes wrong, be part of the solution. Give individuals the same liberty and understanding as you would give yourself.

❖ Go over the requirements of upcoming events with hourly team members in department meetings.

27

A Friendship to Remember

Raahyitha Bakshi thought it was just another routine business trip. When he checked in, he had planned to return to his home in India after two weeks of visiting clients. Never could he have foreseen the drastic turn his journey would take.

The news our general manager delivered in our March staff meeting was unprecedented. "Every group has canceled through June. Cut your staff."

We all left the meeting speechless.

As the coronavirus (COVID-19) spread like wildfire, nations around the globe, including ours, began to close their borders. In turn, every group on the books for our second quarter canceled—one phone call at a time. As business fell through their hands, the perplexed executive committee met daily to strategize a response to this dramatic world event. Managers were promised a game plan within a week.

That same day as I stood at the front desk, Avery, our front desk agent, approached.

"Kim, this gentleman would like to extend his stay. He's been here since February."

I walked over and smiled. "Good morning. My name is Kim." I glanced at the guest's reservation. "May I ask how you pronounce your name?"

"Hi, Kim. Thank you. Everyone calls me RB." His demeanor was calm and pleasant.

"Thank you, RB. We are happy to extend your stay." I began to update his reservation. "What brings you to the area?"

"I was here on a business trip. I was supposed to go home tomorrow, but my country now requires returning citizens to quarantine in a hospital for two weeks. I prefer to stay here and wait it out."

"It's much more comfortable in a hotel, isn't it?" We both laughed.

"RB, I see that we have a suite available. Would you be interested in an upgrade?"

His eyes brightened. "Yes. Thank you."

I handed RB a new room key. "Please let us know if you need anything at all."

With a nod, he retreated to his room.

As promised, the GM called all managers to a meeting the following week. That's when he broke the news. The hotel would remain open with a 90 percent staff reduction. One front desk agent and one security officer per shift would man the property. Two housekeepers would be assigned to clean and sanitize public areas, while guestroom cleaning and all other services ceased. The lobby coffee shop would be our only food and beverage outlet to remain open and serve to-go orders only.

Our four-hundred-room hotel and forty-thousand-square-foot conference center were essentially shut down.

As many countries remained closed, America joined them. City and state governors enforced mandates that progressed from social distancing to wearing masks to self-isolation.

RB's window of opportunity to go home also closed during the two weeks he chose to "wait it out here." He continued to extend his stay one month at a time. During his time with us, he established a friendship with the front desk team. Each morning, he ordered his to-go breakfast in the coffee shop. Then he would walk to the front desk to chat. Since he is a news devotee and I'm not, I'd often ask him for an update on the status of the world. He'd ask what I did on my days off. When he learned I was taking guitar lessons, he asked to hear me play.

"Come on, Kim. There's no one in the entire hotel but you and me." He motioned to the empty lobby. "You can play right here."

As a shy rule follower, I smiled, then changed the subject. "So, how is your family?"

"They are okay. They miss me," he replied.

"Does your bracelet have meaning?" I had noticed it before. Perhaps his answer would help me get to know him better.

He looked at the red strappy band on his wrist. "My seventeen-year-old daughter gave this to me. She asked me to wear it until it falls off. I told her I would."

"Tell me about the rest of your family, RB."

"I have an elderly mother who depends on me greatly," he replied.

"Is she okay?"

"Yes, she is," he assured me.

RB invited me to join him for a drink on several occasions. I knew he was lonely. I yearned to be there for him, but I declined his invitations because it's never wise for a manager to get involved with a guest. Each time, he was gracious and understanding. At one point, he returned late at night after having a few drinks. I asked him where he'd been.

"Out, making myself happy."

At that time, he asked me for my phone number so we could chat by text. Surprised and not knowing what to do, I gave him my work number.

I received two gifts from RB during his stay: a bottle of wine, and then, when he learned I don't drink, a box of gourmet chocolates. RB appreciated everyone at the front desk. He thought Amy was cheerful and funny. She nicknamed him Tom (as in Tom Hanks's character in the movie *The Terminal*) because of the similarities in their situations. He said he thought I was calm and serene. He said Terence was nice but sanitized the front desk too much.

We all went through so much together—the seriousness of the virus, the inexplicable toilet paper shortage, a paper towel and hand sanitizer shortage, and a no haircut crisis.

After four solid months, with occupancy still at rock-bottom levels and little change globally, RB finally secured a flight home.

On Friday, July 3, he approached the front desk. "I have not-so-good news, Kim. I am leaving Sunday."

"That's what I heard, RB," I said sadly. "I am so happy for you."

We both paused.

"I want to tell you again, RB, how much I appreciate you. It has been a pleasure spending this time with you."

His voice softened. "I would like to keep in touch, but you don't seem to answer your text messages, Kim."

I smiled and said, "Let's keep in touch by email, okay?"

"Okay." He nodded and headed toward his room.

The next morning, Amy and I worked together for a small spurt of July 4th business. As I stood a few feet away with another guest, she handed RB a gift from all of us—an attractive T-shirt she found at a local shop that reads "You May Call It Texas, But I Call It Home!" and a card signed by all.

My inscription said:

> *RB,*
>
> *It has been a pleasure having you as our guest for your COVID-19 vacation. You are in our history books!*

RB stepped away with his gift in hand as Amy and I finished with a short line of guests. He walked back over. I overheard him sweetly ask Amy, "Can I hug you guys?"

Seconds later, Amy walked over to me and whispered, "Are you going to hug him, Kim?" We walked toward him. With no regard for social distancing, I opened my arms wide and invited him in. He held tight. So did I.

"Kim," he said softly, "I'm going to miss you, especially."

My eyes filled with tears. *I didn't see that coming.*

"Don't be so formal, okay?" he said.

I turned toward the front desk. Amy and RB followed after they said their goodbyes.

Amy went back to work. RB leaned on the wall near me, "Goodbye, Kim. I will miss you." His eyes spoke louder than his words.

"Goodbye, RB. I will miss you too."

Finally, on July 5, 2020, RB went home.

When I walked into the hotel that afternoon, I was sad to feel his absence.

Hospitality Hints

❖ Let guests know you appreciate them.

❖ Never let emotions overrule good judgment.

❖ No matter what anyone else does, do what is right.

28

No Power, No Generator,
No Problem

The weatherman predicted a record-breaking snowfall over the weekend: six inches within four days. Knowing this would paralyze the city and the nearby airport, we strategized a plan. Twenty essential staff packed our bags, checked in, and braced ourselves for the epic event.

My alarm sounded at 6:00 a.m., one hour before anyone expected me downstairs at the front desk. Since I was only an elevator ride away, I stayed in bed as long as possible. After a sound sleep, I reluctantly slipped from under the warm covers and walked half-awake to the window. Pulling the curtain back confirmed the predicted overnight blizzard. The sun had not yet risen, but the blanket of snow made the dark seem light.

I quickly started getting ready for the day. Nearly dressed, I reached for the hairdryer. Suddenly the room went black.

I froze with hairdryer in hand. *Please come back on.*

I set the hairdryer down, then pawed my way through the dark to the nightstand, found my book light, and did my best to make myself presentable. After ten minutes and still no power, I grabbed my purse, opened the door, shone my book light into the hall, and slowly made my way to the stairwell exit. After pushing the heavy door open, my light and I managed our way down six flights of stairs.

As I exited the stairwell and entered the lobby, I saw the glow from a small lantern at the front desk and Darlene, our night auditor, standing in its shadows.

I spoke softly as I approached. "Good morning, Darlene. No backup generators?"

"The electrical panel is out. Apparently, it isn't made for sub-zero temperatures."

Darlene briefed me on the particulars and assured me she would be safe driving home. After all, she is from up north. I set my purse down but kept my winter coat on. That wasn't usually appropriate, but extraordinary circumstances called for extraordinary measures.

Darlene informed me that according to engineering, our power should be restored by 8:45 a.m.

That time came and went. Still no power.

Mid-morning, when Terence, our assistant front desk manager, came down from his room for his shift, I called our power company rep, Michelle, who gave me an update. "Kim, the automated announcement of 8:45 a.m. restoration was incorrect. Your hotel is not part of the rolling outages. A feeder line is down. We don't know when it will be repaired."

Disappointed, I thanked her and hoped for the best.

Still in the COVID-19 pandemic, most of our guests were a government group of two hundred, and most were being deployed throughout the country and locally to assist with vaccinations. The snowstorm felt like a disaster upon disaster.

Around lunchtime, guests started approaching the front desk with reports of canceled flights and requests to extend their stay. With no way to reprogram their keys, we walked guests up the fire escape to their rooms and used our flashlights and master keys to let them in—every time. The grueling efforts were reminiscent of a previous key system outage.

After sympathizing with a government group guest about the cold inside, she reassured me. "This is like camping in Colorado. Handling disasters is what we do!"

I thanked her for the great attitude.

When evening approached and darkness fell around the hotel, guests used their cell phone lights to make their way to their rooms. Everyone tucked themselves in tight for the long, cold winter night.

We awoke in the morning to another two inches of snow.

Mid-morning, the group's team pulled an SUV in the front drive, ran two thick yellow cables in the front door, and impressively started to charge fifty cell phones at a time.

About that time, local residents started walking in, claiming to have reservations. We realized we were not closed to online bookings as we had thought. I quickly called Jerry, our revenue manager. I could hear his disappointment as he informed me that one hundred reservations were made that we could not honor, for obvious reasons, before he closed the system. Apparently, the bookings were from locals who also had no power.

I sank inside but laughed. "Jerry, you have to see the humor in this. We're in a pandemic, going through a blizzard, our power is out, the generator failed, we have no fail-safe backup keys, and now this. It will be okay, and we will handle it. Just think, next week it will be seventy degrees and back to normal."

I called our power rep again. Michelle was more forthcoming. "Kim, we have to offload a certain amount of power to protect the main grid. Your property is part of the offload. If the grid goes down, it will take up to two weeks to fix."

So it wasn't the feeder line after all.

I spoke kindly with a factual tone. "Michelle, we have two hundred guests in a hotel without power or a backup generator. No lights, no heat. It's forty degrees *inside*. We are walking up pitch-black stairwells. Do you understand what we are going through? Can you at least put us on the *rolling* outages like everyone else?"

She apologized sympathetically and said they were doing their best.

I resisted the temptation to be frustrated and thanked her again.

Remember those one hundred reservations for which we had no rooms? The guests continued to arrive. As they walked in, we broke the news to them, one by one, all day long.

That was fun.

At 2:20 p.m., I found an opportunity to walk down the hall for a moment's peace. Now at the opposite end of the hotel, I approached a cold window and hugged my coat as I looked out and soaked in the silence.

Suddenly, as quickly as it had gone off, the power surged, and the lights came on.

Stunned, I threw up my arms and looked around for someone with which to be excited. I chuckled at the humor of being alone when the power came on. I dashed down the empty hall toward the front desk. I had just missed the eruption of cheers from the people I'd bonded with over the two-day dilemma. I was sorry to have missed that. But I was glad to jump back behind the front desk and get to work on the catch-up process.

To our relief, the power stayed on, and business got back to normal—after hours of catching up the computer system and the repairs of the numerous water-pipe breaks, that is.

The entire hotel staff did an outstanding job of teamwork and service. Our general manager led the way and handled the catastrophe with solid, grounded strength. The food and beverage team was magical in feeding over two hundred people *well* with no lights or heat. And I will never forget the government group's great attitude or the irony of having a *disaster relief group* in-house *during a disaster*.

Hospitality Hints

❖ Keep a positive attitude and a good sense of humor always.

❖ Get good rest. It's your superpower!

❖ Train your staff on how to run the front desk without computers.

❖ Service and inspect your generator regularly.

❖ Check your fail-safe keys regularly.

❖ Have ample lanterns and flashlights at all times.

29

A Not-So-Suite Upgrade

My dear British friend used my employee travel benefit to attend a writer's conference in Tennessee. The unexpected ups and downs of her experience took her on an emotional roller coaster ride. I wasn't present at the time, but she was sure to give me a full rundown about the ordeal on her return.

Jackie, **the front desk agent,** offered a cheerful welcome as my friend approached.

"Good afternoon. My name is Sharon Tedford. I'm checking in for the conference."

"Thank you, Ms. Tedford. Welcome."

After checking the computer, Jackie looked up, "I am happy to inform you that we have upgraded you to the executive floor. Will that be acceptable?"

"Oh. Really?" Sharon was delighted but surprised. "But I'm a guest on my friend's employee discount."

"Yes." Jackie smiled. "And your loyalty status allows me to upgrade you." Jackie was eager to please.

Sharon lit up with excitement. "Thank you."

Jackie assured her that the hotel had plenty of availability as she gave her the room key.

"Thank you, Jackie. You are very kind." Sharon wheeled her

suitcase to the elevator. As she stepped off onto the executive floor, she began to look for room 1061.

Ah, here it is.

PRESIDENTIAL SUITE.

Sharon cocked her head. *This can't be right.* She looked down at her key packet, then up again to verify it was the correct room. *It's the same number. But this can't be it.* Sharon's posture stiffened as her eyes looked to the left, then right. She held the key close as she inched toward the door. *If the light turns red, I'll go back to the front desk.*

She touched the key to the lock. Her eyes brightened to see a green light appear.

Sharon opened the door slowly, peeked in, then stepped inside. She gasped as her eyes scanned the apartment-sized luxury suite. She immediately walked to the phone to call the front desk.

"Hello, Jackie, there must be a mistake. I'm in the *presidential suite.*"

"No, ma'am. There's no mistake. It's on us. Enjoy your stay, Mrs. Tedford."

Sharon hung up the phone. Giddy with excitement, she called her husband, Gareth, on video chat. She took the next ten minutes, sharing the experience with him, going from room to room. "This is where I will dwell the entire weekend."

After her video chat with Gareth, Sharon texted her writing group to update them on her good fortune. "We won't need to go out for dinner tomorrow. We will use my *dining room* instead."

After an enjoyable evening with her group of friends, Sharon tucked herself into her luxurious bed for the night, then drifted off to sleep, smiling as she thought about what she would do with all of the amenities in her suite.

In the dark and stillness of the night, the phone rang.

Sharon jumped awake. *Is there a fire? Is it family overseas? Gareth?* She glanced at the clock as she reached for the phone—1:23 a.m.

"Hello?" She braced herself.

The male voice on the other end of the phone was abrupt. "This is the front desk. Who is this?"

Puzzled and cautious, Sharon replied, "You should know who this is. My name is in your computer. Who is *this*?"

"You shouldn't be in that room!"

"I'm sorry, but I was given this room. I have a key. My name is in your computer. It's Sharon Tedford."

The front desk agent's voice rose to a more fevered pitch. "You shouldn't be there. It's the presidential suite. How did you get there? You're only on employee travel. You need to change rooms."

Sharon was beginning to lose patience. "Okay, but given the hour, must I move *now?*"

There came a huge sigh from the front desk agent. "Well, I suppose it won't hurt if you stay until morning. But I need to see you at the desk first thing."

Wide awake now and more than a bit irritated, Sharon realized this was a hotel mistake, not hers. "Okay. What is your name?"

"Rudy."

"Thank you, Rudy." Click.

Sharon sank back into the pillow. She no longer felt secure and even contemplated putting a dining chair against the doorknob. Instead, she laid back and concentrated on calming herself.

Unable to fall back asleep, Sharon rose early, packed, and was at the front desk by 6:00 a.m., as commanded.

"I'd like to speak to the manager," she kindly informed Julie, the front desk agent.

Julie offered her a smile. "I can help you."

"No." Sharon shook her head. "You won't do. I need to speak to someone in charge, please. There's been an incident I would like to discuss."

Hubert, the front office manager, stepped from behind the front desk and listened closely as Sharon informed him of her unfortunate middle-of-the-night ordeal.

The young manager's countenance sobered. He looked a bit defeated. "I am so sorry. That should *not* have happened to you, Mrs. Tedford. The night auditor should have waited until morning to call. I am sorry he startled you. I have family in Germany, so I understand the situation in great depth. Due to the time difference, if they call in the middle of the night you always think it's an emergency."

"Thank you, Hubert." Sharon appreciated his understanding and compassion.

Hubert continued. "But we will still need to move you, Mrs. Tedford. The guests who reserved the space for their conference arrive today, and they deserve the presidential suite."

Ouch. They deserve it, but I don't?

"Please enjoy breakfast on us. And, because of the inconvenience, your entire stay will be complimentary. Again, my apologies." Hubert was sincere and to the point.

Disappointed but now clear, Sharon thanked Hubert and turned to go to her new room. She exited the elevator, luggage in hand, and walked slowly past her former luxury suite to her new room three doors down the hall. *I don't deserve the suite. How could he say such a thing?*

She touched her key card to the door lock, then entered. Leaving her luggage by the door, she took a quick tour of the room. It was much smaller but comfortable.

Sadly, Sharon spent the next three nights wide awake thanks to her neighbor's loud TV. She called the front desk for help each night, but no one answered.

Rudy must have caller ID.

Hospitality Hints

❖ Implement a policy not to disturb guests between 9:00 p.m. and 9:00 a.m. unless it's critical.

❖ Know the policies regarding employee-associated reservations and upgrades.

❖ Offer the same high level of service to employees and their friends and family.

❖ Be sensitive to all guest's feelings. Choose your words carefully.

❖ If a team member makes a mistake, be honest (but do not give too much information), apologize, and offer to help the guest as you straighten out the issue.

❖ It's never okay to be rude to a guest.

30

A Walk on the Wild Side

My friend Deb did something she hadn't done since she was sixteen years old. Her mother warned her about it when she was a teenager, predicting dire outcomes if she were to ignore her advice. Deb had made a personal commitment to heed her mother's advice all her life. But this night was different.

After a long day of travel, Deb contemplated her options. She knew what the right thing to do was. Still, throwing caution to the wind and feeling a bit of a rebel spirit, Deb indulged herself. She went to bed without removing her makeup.

Now to many of you, that might seem tame—hardly a walk on the wild side. Well, you didn't know Deb's mother.

Deb retired for the night on hotel room sheets, which may have supported her decision, knowing someone else would deal with the rubbed-off foundation and the flecks of mascara. She bravely made a choice and suffered no guilt. She nodded off to sleep quickly and soundly.

Her peaceful rest was shattered at 3:58 a.m. by a piercing, pulsing siren. At first, she believed it to be an emergency vehicle outside her window on the street below. Soon, with the sleep fog lifting, she realized the sound was not outside but inside. It was the shriek of the hotel fire alarm!

"What's the source of the alarm?" Deb asked the moment the operator picked up the phone receiver.

"It's a technical difficulty. Sorry for the disruption."

The operator's response wasn't convincing. Her voice had been uncertain, and Deb had called only moments after the alarm began to ring. *How could the operator possibly know there would be no need for concern so quickly? What if she's wrong?*

Deb heard several doors slam on her floor. A glance into the hall revealed people with coats pulled on over pajamas and hair standing wildly, as though they'd been frightened by the deafening sound. She quickly decided to join them.

Shedding her pajama pants in favor of jeans, Deb jammed her feet into tennis shoes and threw on a coat to make it all respectable. Then she hurried down five flights of stairs to the lobby, fastidiously avoiding the elevators as the signs insisted. Taking the elevator would have been so much easier, but by this time, her rebel spirit was gone, and she followed the instructions to the letter.

By the time Deb reached the lobby, the alarm was silenced, and the crowd of people began to head back to their rooms. She was surprised that more guests had not bothered to come downstairs. Deb noticed her friend and coworker, Jane, who stood in her bathrobe across the room. The two exchanged weird looks. Then with narrowed eyes and a cocked head, Jane looked at Deb as if to say, "What on earth?"

Deb was uncertain of what that look meant and too tired to find out. Separated by the crowd, Deb and Jane turned and headed toward their elevators. The two ladies had a long day ahead of them and needed their rest.

Deb stepped into the bathroom to turn off the light on arrival to her room. When she caught sight of herself in the mirror, she laughed. There she stood, her makeup amazingly intact, no smeared lipstick, no raccoon eyes. She looked as though she had prepared herself for the emergency middle-of-the-night evacuation by painstakingly applying a full range of cosmetics.

No wonder Jane had given her such an odd look.

What were the chances that the one night Deb chose to go rogue, refusing to remove her makeup before bed responsibly, she'd find herself trotting around in public at 4:00 a.m.? She smiled when she thought of the irony.

Before turning off her lamp, Deb looked up and smiled, "Mom, though tonight seemed like it was meant to be, I promise to continue to follow your advice." Then she sunk into her pillow and drifted off to sleep.

Hospitality Hints

❖ Know and follow your hotel's procedures regarding fire alarms and all types of emergencies.

❖ Treat a fire alarm emergency as authentic until confirmed otherwise. Never assume it's another burnt bag of popcorn or a guest smoking in a nonsmoking room.

❖ Stay calm, professional, focused, and in control. Your being at ease will help your team and guests be at ease.

For the Guest

❖ Cooperate with hotel staff. Be kind and understanding. They share the same annoyance with the alarm as you do. The difference is that they can't show it.

❖ Know that it's okay to ask questions.

❖ Remain calm.

Epilogue

Is the hotel industry all laughs? Certainly not. But it can be a fun and rewarding career. It's all about your attitude and outlook. There's something to that question, "Is the glass half full or half empty?" What is *your* approach? I'm not talking about the thin veneer of forced happiness. This is about that solid foundation of knowing things always work out and letting that confidence show to the point of influence.

When you join a hotel, you join a family. There will be many different personalities. Not everyone's sense of humor will be like yours. For these reasons and more, it's important to develop good people skills—and to know ahead of time how you will respond in good scenarios and challenging ones.

Show interest in others. Learn to listen. Be easygoing. You've heard it before, and it's worth saying again: the hotel industry is not rocket science. It's all about people and relationships. Develop and grow those two things, add a good work ethic, and you have tapped into the secret to hospitality success.

Hotels have many rules. Most of them are guidelines. At my property, I let my team know that there are only two black-and-white policies:

1.   The guest must pay for the room. "No pay, no stay."

2.   The guest's information is kept confidential. No exception. "No ID, no key."

Other than those two, the team is empowered to make decisions after proper training. They receive the ability to practice the art of hospitality. What is the *art* of hospitality? Just as a painter chooses the right brush stroke or adds a special touch to his masterpiece, the hotelier must know what works in a particular interaction. What is that special touch that will make your interaction its best?

Every hotel has something special and unique about its property. But it's the people that keep the guests coming back. Are you someone the guest looks forward to seeing again? Have you made an effort to make their stay memorable (above average)? It's much easier for your sales department if they don't have to go out and find new business every week. Take good care of the guests, and they will return again and again. Because of the service you provide, your hotel will sell itself.

General managers, stay involved. You are wanted and needed. Walk your hotel. Talk to the team members. Shake their hands. Have regular meetings with groups of employees from all departments. Yes, payroll is a hotel's most significant expense, but it's also its biggest asset. Don't skimp here. Overworking or overloading employees will hurt service and damage the bottom line. Keep the guests coming back and the service adjustments away by prioritizing staffing, training, and recognition. Listen and observe everyone. Know that you set the tone.

And always remember to smile, laugh, and have fun!

Section Topics

Attitude and Integrity

Guest Interaction

Management

Relationship

Safety and Security

Glossary of Terms and Acronyms

AFOM – Assistant front office manager

AGM – Assistant general manager

Amenity – A desirable item, such as food, given to a guest by hotel staff; usually sent to the guest's room

Comp – Complimentary

Concierge – A person or service that provides assistance with personal business (such as making travel arrangements, scheduling appointments, or running errands)[3]

F&B – Food and beverage

FOM – Front office manager

GM – General manager

Gratuity – A tip (usually monetary)

Hot box – A portable box used to carry food pans to and from a catered event or banquet

HR – Human resources

HRM – Hotel and restaurant management

Lobby lizard – Slang for lobby ambassador; a person who oversees the lobby

MOD – Manager on duty

Motel – A combination of "motor hotel," this is a kind of hotel that is generally cheaper and with less frills; most often rooms are accessible from the outside, not from within a central lobby

No Show – A guest that fails to check in for a guaranteed reservation

PBX – Private Branch Exchange. A switchboard the telephone operator uses

TMI – Too much information

Transient guest – A guest who stays briefly; typically non-group

VIP – Very important person

Notes

1 Zig Zigler, *Top Performance: How to Develop Excellence in Yourself and Others* (Grand Rapids: Revell, 2019).

2 Jeanne Robertson, *Don't Let the Funny Stuff Get Away: Turn Everyday Experiences Into Stories That Audiences Will Remember!* (Houston: Rich Pub Co, 1998).

3 *Merriam-Webster's Collegiate Dictionary*, s.v. "concierge," accessed June 1, 2022, https://unabridged.merriam-webster.com/collegiate/concierge.

About the Author

Kimberly Annington's career consists of leadership positions in multiple outstanding hotels. She is an award-winning manager who has worked across brands for thirty years and is a seasoned, well-versed hospitality industry veteran. She has collected knowledge and know-how from her experience in award-winning properties.

As a student at the "University of Hard Knocks" in hospitality, Kimberly has progressed through career opportunities into upper-level management roles. She offers both her hard-won insight and encouragement to others to persevere and savor the exciting world of hospitality.

After traveling all over the US while growing up, Kimberly's family settled in the great state of Texas, which she calls home. She and her dog, Lucy, live in a Dallas suburb. Her hobbies are gardening, guitar, and writing.